TEN-MINUTE
TRANSFORMATION

TEN-MINUTE
TRANSFORMATION

SMALL SPIRITUAL STEPS THAT REVOLUTIONIZE YOUR LIFE

Chris Altrock

CHALICE
PRESS
ST. LOUIS, MISSOURI

Cover image: iStock photo
Cover design: Scribe, Inc.

Visit www.chalicepress.com

10 9 8 7 6 5 4 3 2 1   13   14   15   16   17   18

Print: 9780827237063   EPUB: 9780827237070   EPDF: 978827237087

**Library of Congress Cataloging-in-Publication Data
available upon request**

Printed in the United States of America

This book is dedicated to my son Jacob and my daughter Jordan.
My goal was to write a book that might inspire you
(and others like you) toward higher degrees of holiness.
Just as you have stirred me toward greater godliness
while you've lived at home, I pray this book will stir you
as you launch out to pursue God's dreams for you.
These are the most important principles and practices
I've learned about life with God.
May they become yours as well.

Contents

Acknowledgments ix

Section One: Living on Purpose

Chapter 1: Little Is the New Big 1

Chapter 2: What's Your Sentence? 11

Chapter 3: Living for the World's Sake 17

Chapter 4: Four Principles of Life Change 22

Section Two: Genuine in Piety

Chapter 5: Swimming beyond the Shallow End 34

Chapter 6: Unforgetting God 40

Chapter 7: Identifying Your Invisible Iniquity 43

Chapter 8: Praying at Different Elevations 47

Chapter 9: Talking to the Father Like the Son 51

Chapter 10: Using Paul's Pre-Owned Prayers 57

Chapter 11: Hearing Heaven's Voice 61

Chapter 12: Reading for Change 65

Chapter 13: Direction from Above 68

Chapter 14: Putting an End to Words 71

Chapter 15: Saving the Most Endangered Species 76

Chapter 16: Finding Power in a Pause 83

Section Three: Gracious toward People

Chapter 17: Placing Relationships Back into Religion 90

Chapter 18: Becoming a Secret Service Agent 93

Chapter 19: Getting Rid of Self-Service 96

Chapter 20: Confessing Your Way to Compassion 99

Chapter 21: Seeing Yourself Through the Eyes of Others 102

Chapter 22: Eliminating Counterfeit Confession 105

Chapter 23: Treating Your Hurry Sickness 108

Chapter 24: Growing by Slowing 111

Chapter 25: The Ministry of Marinating. 114

Chapter 26: Shifting Your Center of Gravity 117

Chapter 27: Packing Your Prayer Closet. 120

Chapter 28: The Greatest Need of Others 124

Section Four: Generous with Possessions

Chapter 29: Dodging the Dark Side 128

Chapter 30: Spreading Good News by Sharing Good Food . . 132

Chapter 31: Moving Like Jesus 135

Chapter 32: Changing Your Focus 139

Chapter 33: Making God's Presence Your Greatest Possession 142

Chapter 34: Finding God in Your Backyard 146

Chapter 35: Taking the Remedy of Simplicity 151

Chapter 36: Giving Up the Good Life 156

Chapter 37: Uncluttering Your Heart 160

Chapter 38: Putting Happiness Back into Holiness 164

Chapter 39: Practicing Joy Like Jesus 168

Chapter 40: Praising in Phases. 172

Chapter 41: Living Large. 176

Appendix 181

Notes. 185

Acknowledgments

I am grateful for the many at the Highland Church of Christ in Memphis, Tennessee, who pursue spiritual formation for the glory of God and for the good of others. Whether empowering the unemployed through HopeWorks, blessing orphans and families through Agape, or serving others in Ukraine, you demonstrate spirituality designed to make the world a better place. The substance of this book came from observing God at work in you.

SECTION ONE

Living on Purpose

1

Little Is the New Big

Many years ago my friend Joe Cannon was preaching in a remote village in the Chimbu Mountains of Papua New Guinea. Suddenly hundreds of angry tribesmen surrounded him. One wild-looking bushman held a sharp axe and screamed in his native tongue, "Do you see this axe? If you are here tomorrow morning, I'm going to give it to you!" Joe, with characteristic humor, later wrote, "This was the first time in my life when the promise of a gift made me nervous." Despite the threat on his life, Joe continued preaching in the village.

The next morning the same angry mob circled Joe like lions circling their prey. The man with the axe stepped forward and sprinted at Joe–axe raised high and his face fixed in an ancient tribal expression of intimidation. Joe's life was about to end on this isolated island thousands of miles from his home.

At the last moment, another tribesman rushed in front of the axe-wielding bushman. Weeks earlier Joe had baptized this rescuer into Christ. The man pleaded with the assailant, "Kill me instead! Kill me instead!" That stunning act stopped the axe man in his tracks. In the face of such sacrifice, the tribe decided that Joe would not die. His life would be spared.

Joe and the gospel won. Many from the tribe were eventually led to faith in Christ.

This is one of dozens of Bible-like accounts from the life of Joe Cannon. He's come closer to living out stories from Acts and elsewhere in Scripture than anyone else I know. As a former staff member in the congregation I preach for, Joe's always been larger than life to me. His impact and influence around the world have been immeasurable.

But this mighty man had mighty small beginnings. Joe spent his early years in Canada in a street gang. Teachers, neighbors, and peers who knew him in his teens in the 1930s might have imagined that the only future he had was one of crime and punishment. He was on the road to ruin, certain to become a nobody. Yet God broke into Joe's life, changed his heart, and gave him a calling that would take him to four foreign fields and a ministry that would span sixty years.

The journey from humble beginnings to heavenly impact began in Japan. Immediately after World War II a new wave of missionaries was entering this wartorn land. Among this flood of eager and enthusiastic ministers were Joe Cannon and his wife Rosabelle. Joe once described to me his decision to go to Japan: "I believe Jesus wanted me to serve among the most unloved people I could find. And at that time, the most unloved people were the Japanese." Joe, Rosabelle, and their family ministered there for twenty-four years. They baptized thousands, planted fifteen churches, and strengthened countless followers of Jesus. Additionally, they played key roles in establishing Ibaraki Christian College, starting four kindergartens, and launching four orphanages.

In 1971 Joe and his family moved from Japan to Papua New Guinea. Joe was the first American missionary among the tribes who lived on these six hundred islands. Knowing one man could never reach all of these natives, Joe decided on a model in which he would train others to preach and reach. He thus began the Melanesian Bible College in Lae, and then assisted in the establishment of similar schools. He served at the Bible college for thirteen years, leading future church-planters to Christ and then training them to return to their villages to do the same. Hundreds of churches were planted through Joe's efforts.

In 1983 Joe and Rosabelle moved to Memphis, Tennessee, to launch a training program called Mission 1000. Hosted at the Highland Church of Christ where I preach, Mission 1000 aimed to recruit, train, and send one thousand para-missionaries to support mission work around the globe. Hundreds of men and women were eventually equipped and commissioned to assist foreign mission efforts. During this same time period Joe and Rosabelle made annual trips to Irian Jaya, Indonesia, to establish yet another pioneer work among unreached tribes.

After the death of his wife Rosabelle, Joe married Betty Dollar. Betty had left her full-time work as a realtor in Memphis to share Jesus in Ukraine. Ukraine, which had become independent from the former Soviet Union in 1991, was the breadbasket of its region. And, in the early 1990s, there was a spiritual harvest from this breadbasket: tens of thousands of Bibles were distributed, several thousand people were baptized, and many congregations were planted. Betty joined this surge of mission work in 1995 and helped establish the Bila Tserkva Church of Christ. For many years she labored there with other missionaries. Joe joined her when they married in 2002.

When in Ukraine, Joe and Betty taught non-Christians and Christians at the church building and in their apartment seven days a week. They ministered to teenagers at the Shans Center, which served youth who suffered from multiple sclerosis, spina bifida, and other illnesses. During Joe and Betty's time in Bila Tserkva, more than a hundred people of all ages were baptized.

Joe once wrote about his world-shaping ministry:

> Pioneering with the gospel! This is the great thrill of missionary work... Bringing souls to Christ who have never heard of Him before. Reaching people with the gospel who never had a chance before... In missionary life, you go by faith into the unknown. You bet your life on the promises and providence of God... What a joy to this happy pioneer to arrive in strange places, and find Christ is there... To meet the challenges, to have every fiber of your soul and personality tested and tried. To be purified by the ups and downs, the successes and failures, the joy and sorrow... To be in the place where victories are won against seeming overwhelming odds. What can take the place of experiences like this?... This is the life for me![1]

What strikes me most about Joe's story is how it began in such a small way. The final chapters of his story reveal a ministry of unparalleled breadth and depth—thousands saved, dozens of churches planted, numerous schools started, hundreds of Christian leaders trained, and scores of the neglected loved and blessed. But the first chapter in his story reveals just a teenage boy in a gang—a boy who did not worship God. There couldn't be a greater contrast than the one between the first and last chapters of this epic adventure. God took a small and humble beginning and did something vast and significant with it.

But that's normal for God.

Little and Big in God's Kingdom

We can view Joe's story as a parable that shows the way God tends to work in the world. Jesus said God's kingdom is like a man who plants a mustard seed–the smallest of seeds–and watches it grow into a large tree (Mt. 13:31–32). Jesus taught that if a God-follower has a tiny amount of faith–as small as a mustard seed–God can do tremendous things with it (Mt. 17:19–21). God makes a habit of taking the small and doing the significant. His practice is to take the miniature and do the massive.

Consider the first followers of Jesus. Their numbers and social standing were miniscule. But their impact was mighty. As Jesus scanned the group who'd gathered near him prior to delivering his Sermon on the Mount, he saw people with no one in their corner, people weary of all that was wrong in the world, people missing out on the best of life, and people hungering for the world to be made right (Mt. 5:2–12). He saw the poor...the mournful...the meek...the hungry and thirsty. There could hardly be a group of smaller and more humble people.

But he told them, "You are the salt of the earth... You are the light of the world" (Mt. 5:13–16). This crowd of the fringe and the forgotten would do big things. They would drive out decay and darkness everywhere around them. And their influence would be felt–not just in Jerusalem, not only in Israel or the Roman Empire. They would affect "the earth." They would change "the world." Their numbers and social standing were miniscule, but their impact would be massive.

In God's world, little is the new big.

That's what this book is about. It's about a God who can take the little and do the large. We've seen him do it again and again. For example, few in Christian history have had as immense an impact on the world as the woman known as Mother Teresa. She once spoke about her influence: "I don't do big things. I do small things with big love."[2] Her life was a tidal wave of mercy and compassion. Yet the wave comprised small drops, tiny acts done here and there. It's inspiring the way God can take a little and do a lot.

In God's world, little is the new big.

The Little Big Jesus

Not only can something big come from something small, but something heavenly can result from something humble. Jesus reveals this in a speech at the end of John 6. The topic of the speech is what Jesus calls "bread...from heaven" (vv. 31, 32, 33, 41, 50, 51, and 58). This phrase is his way of describing how God is going to do something heavenly on earth. The kingdom is about to come. Heaven is about to plant a flag on earth. God is going to break into human history in a transformative way.

What is that going to look like? What is this "bread from heaven," and what is it going to do?

Jesus says this bread will…

- bring eternal life (vv. 27, 51)
- give life to the world (v. 33)
- eliminate hunger and thirst (v. 35)
- make possible life after death (v. 40)
- lead to spiritual intimacy (v. 56)

This is pretty heavenly stuff. The bread from heaven is life-giving and healing. Jesus' speech at the end of John 6 is about how God's doing something so heavenly that it's going to result in a better life for every person on the planet.

Imagine a meeting that might have taken place before this speech. God gathers his best thinkers and says, "I need you to come up with a device that can bring about heavenly results on earth. This apparatus must be capable of bringing life to every person on the planet. It must eliminate hunger and thirst. It must make possible life after death. It must lead to spiritual intimacy. I'm calling this tool 'bread' because humans are so used to thinking about how bread sustains life. But I'm going to leave the form up to you. Come up with a tool that can do this heavenly work on earth." God gives them a week to create their plans.

What might they return with? They might present an earth-sized defibrillator that can jolt life back into the human race. They might propose a needle the size of Texas by which life-giving medicine can be injected into humanity.

But here's the winning entry:

"Jesus said to them, 'I am the bread of life…'" (Jn. 6:35).

"I am the bread of life" (v. 48).

"I am the living bread that came down from heaven" (v. 51).

Jesus says, in essence, "I am that device. I am the means by which God will bring about this life-change. I am the apparatus through which God is bringing heaven on earth."

And some of those listening laugh out loud. They shake their heads and dismiss Jesus as a waste of their time: "So the Jews grumbled about him, because he said, 'I am the bread that came down from heaven.' They said, 'Is not this Jesus, this son of Joseph, whose father and mother we know? How does he now say, 'I have come down from heaven'?" (Jn. 6:41–42).

These people find it impossible to believe that anything heavenly could result from someone as humble as Jesus. After all, this is Jesus!

They watched him grow up. They saw him stumble over a rock as a toddler. They could tell you all kinds of rumors about his parents. He was just a local nut. "Is this not Jesus, this son of Joseph, whose father and mother we know? How does he now say, 'I have come down from heaven'?" There's no way God could do any kind of lasting work through this kind of lowly person.

Yet that's what Jesus claims. Through this "nobody," God would do the kind of things that would change the world. Especially when it came to Jesus, little was the new big.

God does the heavenly through the humble.

God accomplishes the massive through the miniscule.

God achieves the large through the little.

God carries out the significant through the small.

Little and Big in the World

This way that God acts has been woven into the fabric of his creation. Kyle MacDonald's story illustrates this.[3] Kyle was unemployed and unable to provide for himself and Dominique, the love of his life. One day, while staring at the red paperclip holding his resume together, he hatched a crazy plan. He would try to trade that paperclip for something bigger and better, and he would keep trading until he got a house. That's right—Kyle dreamed of eventually trading a paper clip for a house.

He placed an ad on Craigslist in which he offered to swap his paper clip. A woman in Vancouver contacted him, indicating she'd give him a pen for the clip. Kyle then traded the pen for a doorknob. The doorknob got him a camping stove. He swapped the camping stove for an electric generator. The generator led to a neon sign and a keg of beer, which he then exchanged for a snowmobile. Within a year, through trades, swaps, and exchanges, Kyle was finally able to trade for a house in Kipling, Saskatchewan. It all began with one little red paperclip. God has created an entire world in which the small can lead to the big.

Here's yet another example of this truth. Researchers in Taiwan recently endeavored to determine the minimal amount of exercise that would reap health benefits.[4] The study wasn't an attempt to excuse laziness or poor priorities. Those in charge of the study merely wished to learn whether or not even small amounts of exercise could lead to significant results. Here's what they found: just fifteen minutes of exercise a day can lead to a longer life. The study found that people who exercised fifteen minutes a day cut their risk of death by 14 percent and extended their life expectancy by three years compared with people who engaged in no exercise at all. God's world is one in which the tiny can lead to the tremendous.

Malcolm Gladwell writes about the 75th precinct in New York City.[5] He describes it as "an economically desperate community destined, by most accounts, to get more desperate in the years ahead." The precinct was especially infamous for its high crime rate. Yet, during a two-year period, the 75th experienced a miraculous decrease in crime: in 1993, there were 126 homicides; two years later there were only 44. The community was transformed. Gladwell describes the result: "On the streets of the Seven-Five today, it is possible to see signs of everyday life that would have been unthinkable in the early nineties. There are now ordinary people on the streets at dusk—small children riding their bicycles, old people on benches and stoops, people coming out of the subways alone."

What happened? How could crime drop so much? Most people looked for large causes to explain the equally large effect. However, Gladwell writes that the cause was probably something relatively small. The community transformation was eventually explained by the Broken Window Hypothesis. This hypothesis resulted from a famous experiment conducted about thirty years ago by Stanford University psychologist Philip Zimbardo. Zimbardo drove a car to a street in Palo Alto, California. He parked it and left it there for a week. Nothing happened to the car. It remained untouched. No vandalism. No attempts to steal it. Then Zimbardo returned to the car and smashed out one window with a sledgehammer. Again, Zimbardo left the car parked on the street. This time, however, the car with the smashed window was stripped bare by vandals.[6]

Gladwell explains why this happened: "Zimbardo's point was that disorder invites even more disorder—that a small deviation from the norm can set into motion a cascade of vandalism and criminality. The broken window was the tipping point." Negatively, the Broken Window Hypothesis states that if you introduce one small element of disorder (a broken car widow), it can lead to larger disorder (the entire car being stripped). Positively, the hypothesis states that if you address one small element of disorder (e.g., fix a broken window), it can quickly lead to the elimination and prevention of larger disorders.

And that, Gladwell suggests, is what happened in the 75th precinct. Officers began implementing a series of small efforts, such as confiscating more guns, running off more groups who were loitering on street corners, and stopping more suspicious looking cars. Symbolically, they started fixing the broken windows in the community. This led to a drop in larger and more serious crime.

Gladwell concludes, "Sometimes the most modest of changes can bring about enormous effects. What happened to the murder rate may not be such a mystery in the end. Perhaps what [these officers] have done is the equivalent of repairing the broken window." *The most modest of changes can bring about enormous effects.* In other words, the elimination of relatively small offenses by the police led ultimately to a reduction in major crime.

God has created a world in which little is the new big.

I've experienced this in my own life. Three of the six books I've authored (including this one) were written thirty minutes at a time. Because of my congregational ministry, family responsibilities, and other duties, I could only find thirty minutes a day to write. At first I felt like giving up. I thought what I really needed was a few months off to immerse myself in nonstop writing. Thirty minutes was hardly enough time to write an entire book. Most days I could only crank out a couple of paragraphs. On some days I could only write a couple of sentences. But I kept at it. Day after day. Thirty-minute block after thirty-minute block. Eventually those miniature spans of time produced three books.

Little is the new big.

That's the kind of God we have and the kind of world he's created.

Little and Big and Your Spiritual Life

This reality has implications for your spiritual life. For example, a recent study finds that the average American spends about ten minutes per day in religious or spiritual activities.[7] On the one hand, this is bad news. It can be difficult to experience authentic spiritual transformation or genuine spiritual intimacy if all you give it is ten minutes a day. It can seem impossible to affect world change through spiritual actions done ten minutes at a time.

But on the other hand, could these ten minutes be leveraged? Given the way our God does the massive with the miniscule, could God do tremendous things with just ten minutes? Could these tiny moments be a mustard seed that God grows into something amazing?

I believe he can do that. I'm not saying that ten minutes is all God wants. What he wants is every minute of every day. And I'm not saying that ten minutes is all you'll ever need to join him in changing yourself and your world. In the end, it takes every second on the clock and every cell in the body . But I am saying that ten minutes is a great place to start. God is the kind of God who can do more with ten minutes than you ever thought possible.

So here's my challenge: give God ten minutes a day over the next forty days. Be consistent. Be disciplined. Don't compromise. Spend ten minutes every day for forty days in focused and intense spiritual activity. Heavenly things will happen.

To help you make the most of this time, I'll share twelve spiritual activities than can be practiced in these ten-minute segments. I've chosen these twelve spiritual exercises because each can be done in about ten minutes. Though they are brief, they will have an unmistakable impact on your life and your world.

I've also chosen these twelve spiritual habits because each can empower you to fulfill a very specific vision. In this book, we will not focus on "spiritual growth" in general, or on "transformation" in general. We'll focus on achieving a specific dream for our lives and our world–a dream given to us by Jesus himself. Jesus has a stunning portrait of what your life and your world could look like if you lived in deep devotion to God. The portrait comes from his Sermon on the Mount. His vision encompasses three things:

- *People* (our relationships with other people)
- *Piety* (our relationship with God)
- *Possessions* (our approach toward and use of money and goods).[8]

The twelve spiritual practices in this book will help you live into this vision.

In the rest of section 1, each chapter will lead you in a ten-minute exercise that invites Jesus to impress on your heart his dream for your life. These exercises will lead you, ten minutes at a time, in understanding and embracing his three-fold vision for your piety, people, and possessions.

In the remaining sections of this book, we'll explore the twelve exercises through which we can move toward this vision. We'll practice four spiritual disciplines that will deeply affect our *piety* (section 2), four disciplines that will powerfully impact our *people* (section 3), and four disciplines that will radically influence our *possessions* (section 4). You'll spend three days in each ten-minute discipline before moving on to the next one. Thus, in sections 2 through 4, you'll spend twelve days focused solely on reaching for Jesus' dream for your relationship with God (piety), twelve more days spent working toward Jesus' dream for your relationships with others (people), and twelve additional days striving for his dream for your right relationship with money and goods (possessions).

Little is the new big.

So spend ten minutes a day in these spiritual exercises. You'll experience important changes in your intimacy with God, the way you treat others, and your approach toward money.

I hope that these ten minutes will turn out to be just the beginning for you. I pray they'll be a step towards entire days and nights dedicated to living out Jesus' dream.

This isn't a quick-fix book. I won't promise you'll become a Joe Cannon or a Mother Teresa. But I can promise that God takes the small and does the big. I can say with conviction that any journey begins with a step. And these ten minutes could be the most important step you'll ever take.

2

What's Your Sentence?

According to philosopher and spiritual life writer Dallas Willard, there are three steps to achieving significant growth in your life.[9] Whether you are trying to learn Ukrainian for an upcoming business trip to Kiev, become more patient with your two-year-old who has redefined the "terrible two's," or improve your ability to hear guidance from God about an important decision, three steps are required. Willard summarizes them with the letters V, I, M.

First, you have to be able to see a compelling and inspiring **V**ision for the kind of growth you desire. You've got to be able to picture what life could be like if you achieved that goal. This vision becomes the fuel for the engine of transformation.

Next, you need to make an **I**ntentional decision that you're going to pursue this dream. It is never enough just to have a vision. At some point you must make an explicit decision to turn the vision into reality.

Finally, you must determine the **M**eans for living out that vision. This final step sets apart those who merely have a dream and those who actually live it out. You must engage in the difficult work of determining the steps, procedures, habits, and practices that will transform the vision into reality.

Vision

Willard explains VIM with the example of learning a new language. This journey begins with a vision of what life would be like if you learned a new language, and why the cost of learning it will be worth the price. Just thinking, "It'd be neat to know another language," or, "I'll be able to impress others by learning a new language," won't be a vision large enough to sustain you through the difficulties of learning a language. In fact, it's the lack of an adequate vision that explains why so many Americans never learn another language. We literally can't "see" how our lives would be better through acquiring such knowledge. But it is the presence of a compelling vision that explains why many in other nations aspire to learn another language such as English.

For example, my brother Craig has spent decades teaching conversational English in foreign countries. In every city in every country where he and his team open a conversational English school, they are flooded with locals hungry to learn. Why? Because these people have a clear image of the opportunities that will be theirs when they are finally able to speak English. Learning the language can open up to them numerous new educational and economic breaks.

Intention

Next, you make an intentional decision to purse this goal. You stop daydreaming about "Someday" and start thinking about "Today." You transition from, "One day I'm going to learn that language," to, "Right now I'm going to take the first step–whatever that is." The world contains plenty of dreamers. It holds few, however, who have made an intentional decision to live a dream.

For example, I have a list I review regularly called "Goals." This list is filled with things I'd like to do at some point during my life (e.g., tour the Holy Land, spend forty days at a monastery, get a Ph.D., etc.). Some of those items have been on my list for decades. They've never transitioned from a "Goals" list to a "Completed" list. Why? Not because I don't have a compelling vision for them, but because I've never finally and firmly decided, "Starting today I'm going to do whatever it takes to make that goal a reality." I've not made an intentional decision to do whatever I must to live these dreams. For our dreams to become realized, we must choose to make them real.

Means

Finally, having reached this intentional decision, you then map out the means required to learn the language. You devise a specific way in which you will learn a language and a timeframe in which you will learn it. This may involve researching top-rated language software for computers or language schools with good reviews. You might talk to others who have learned the language to find out what resources they recommend. Then you pay the deposit at the language school.

Or you schedule your first appointment with a language instructor. Or you go online and order the computer software. Vision. Intention. Means. All three steps are critical for any meaningful change or growth in life.

Jesus' Vision for Your Life

But growth begins with Vision. And no one has a clearer or more compelling vision for your life than Jesus. In his Sermon on the Mount, he shares this dream. There are at least three reasons why the Sermon on the Mount is the best place to turn for understanding Jesus' vision for your life.

First, Matthew organizes his novel about Jesus around five notable speeches he gave. Matthew believed we could learn a lot about Jesus through these speeches. The first and thus the most important speech is the one Jesus gave that we now call the Sermon on the Mount. For Matthew, this speech is part of the way he summarized what was most important in Jesus' preaching.

Second, Matthew prefaces this speech with language in Matthew 4:23 that tells us that this speech was the best example of the kind of teaching Jesus was doing in his ministry. This Sermon on the Mount is Jesus at his best.

Third, there is a strong correlation between the Ten Commandments in the Old Testament and the Sermon on the Mount in the New Testament. Just as Moses ascended a mount to receive the Ten Commandments, so Jesus ascends a mount to give these commandments. The Ten Commandments focused on our relationship to God ("You shall have no other gods before me..."), our relationship with others ("Honor your father and mother..."), and our relationship with possessions ("You shall not covet your neighbor's goods..."). Similarly, the Sermon on the Mount focuses on the same three areas of life.

In fact, one way of summarizing the whole sermon is to hear it as Jesus' call for us to become gracious toward people, genuine in our piety, and generous in our possessions. If Jesus could have his way with your life, here's what he'd love to see on your tombstone: "___ was gracious toward people, genuine in piety, and generous with possessions." That's the Sermon on the Mount in one sentence. That's Jesus' vision for your life.

Growth and change in any of these three areas begins by firmly fixing Jesus' vision in our minds and hearts. I'm not sure what you imagine when you try to envision the kind of life for which you were created, but here's Jesus' dream for you. Read it slowly. Read it prayerfully. Try to picture each of these lessons:

Genuine in Your Piety

- Practice a faith that is not merely external and superficial (Mt. 5:8).
- Be willing to pay any price to do what's right by God (5:10).
- Live the kind of life God can use as salt and light (5:13–16).
- Give to the poor, pray, and fast for God's sake, not yours (6:1–6, 16–18).
- Pray for *God's* kingdom to come instead of praying for *your* will to be done (6:7–15).
- Trust in a God who knows how to give good gifts (7:7–11).
- Let your path not be the crowded one, but rather the little-traveled one (7:13–14).
- Do not aspire to the claim of sensational spirituality, but rather to the claim of simple obedience (7:21–23).
- Do not merely listen to God's words, but rather live them out (7:24-27).

Gracious Toward People

- Show favor to: the poor in spirit who have no one but God in their corner, the mournful so weary of the wrong in the world, the meek and those missing out, and those who are hungering and thirsting for the world to be made right (Mt. 5:2–6).
- Demonstrate mercy (5:7).
- Pursue God's peace for all people (5:9).
- Do not harbor anger, but rather [there are a lot of "rather's" in this list now – can you alternate with synonyms of rather, or eliminate it altogether?] seek reconciliation (5:21–26).
- Pay any price to think and act without lust (5:27–30).
- Do not divorce, but rather be faithful (5:31–32).
- Do not deceive, but rather let your "yes" mean "yes" (5:33–37).
- Do not respond to evil with violence, but rather with love (5:38–48).
- Pursue the strengthening of your own weaknesses rather than pointing out the weaknesses of others (7:1-6).
- Do to others what you would have them do to you (7:12).
- Do not listen to others because of the fruit on their resumes, but rather because of the fruit in their character (7:15–20).

Generous with Possessions

- Do not be miserly and serve Money, but rather be generous and serve God (Mt. 6:19–24).
- Do not worry, but rather trust in the caring provision and kingdom purpose of God (6:25–34).

Think of your life as a car. On the interior dashboard are three dials. The dial on the left measures the depth of your intimacy with God (piety). The dial in the middle tracks the quality of your relationships with the folks around you (people). The dial on the right indicates the degree to which you are owned by what you own and the level of your generosity toward others (possessions). Optimum readings on all three dials are critical for the car to run as it was created to run.

Think of the world as a patient. In order to determine the patient's health, doctors would run three tests. Test 1 indicates the level of authentic spirituality (piety). Test 2 measures the presence of hatred, intolerance, mercy, or compassion (people). Test 3 provides needed information on the amount of greed and giving going on in the world (possessions). Making the world a better place means increasing fitness in all three areas.

Jesus' vision for life is summarized in these three areas. And movement toward this life begins with impressing his vision upon our hearts. Intentional decisions and mapping out the means will come later. Right now, what matters most is grasping Jesus' vision.

But how do we do that? How do we exchange our alternative visions for Jesus' vision? How do we brand his dream upon our souls?

What's Your Sentence?

Daniel Pink, author of *Drive,* provides a practical answer to these questions.[10] Pink released a video on New Year's Day in 2010 asking the simple question, "What's Your Sentence?"[11] He urged readers and viewers to summarize the purpose of their life in one sentence. They were to write the sentence as if a friend were writing it after the person had died (e.g., Chris loved others deeply; Craig never lied; Jeff made children happy). This sentence becomes a focal point that clarifies priorities and inspires behavior and growth.

As part of a silent retreat in Mobile, Alabama, I was led to spend an afternoon in an old cemetery. Though established officially in 1844, many of the graves there were much older. There were tombstones memorializing infants, teenagers, young adults, middle-aged adults, and people much older. Death had not been choosey. Death had hit them all.

Some markers attempted to summarize the person's life, or something important to that person. For example, Vernon Fowlkes was remembered for loving his family, playing his dulcimer, and drinking malt scotch whiskey! Mary Lucy McKnight was remembered simply as "A best friend." It was said of Presiding Circuit Judge Joseph Hocklande, "He lived as he died, with dignity and courage." Mary Owen's tombstone remarked, "She loved everyone and saw good in everything."

These are the kinds of sentences Daniel Pink urges us to consider. So, imagine you are at a funeral–your funeral. Three people have each been asked to share one sentence that encapsulates your life. The first shares one sentence about the level of your piety. The second shares one sentence that speaks about how you treated people. The third recites one sentence that sums up your approach toward possessions.

What are these three sentences? What is your life going to be about when it comes to piety, people, and possessions? What one thing do you hope people will remember after your death regarding your relationship with God? What one thing do you dream of others saying after your death about your relationships with others? What one thing do you wish people will record about you when it comes to your view of and use of money?

TAKE ⑩

Take ten minutes today to write these three sentences. This exercise will clarify a vision for your life. That's the first step in experiencing real change in your world and in the world around you.

Piety_____.

People_____.

Possessions_____.

3

Living for the World's Sake

The Power of a Life Well Lived

Chinese officials grew troubled in the 1990s at the sight of persistent crime, drug addiction, and sickness in the Yunnan province.[12] For assistance, they turned to the only exemplary citizens they could locate among the people of that region. They hoped these model citizens might assert some positive peer pressure on others. One Chinese official spoke anonymously:

> We had to admit that the Lahu people were a dead loss because of their addiction to opium... Their addiction made them weak and sick. Then they would go to one of their "priests," who required animal sacrifices of such extravagance that the people became poor. And because they were so poor, they stole from each other, and law and order deteriorated. It was a vicious cycle that no amount of government propaganda could break. We noticed, however, that in some villages in the country, the Lahu were prosperous and peace loving. There was no drug problem or any stealing or social order problems. Households had a plentiful supply of pigs, oxen, and chickens. So we commissioned a survey to find out why these villages were different. To our astonishment and embarrassment, we discovered the key factor was that these villages had a majority of Christians.

Some villages manufactured only chaos and crime. Others produced peace and prosperity. The latter seemed due to the influence of Christians. To test this, the officials took a risky gamble. They asked a group of Christians to move into one of the drug-addicted and poverty-stricken villages. There, the Christians were to spread their alternative lifestyle. Jumping at the chance, Christians transplanted themselves into the village and began sharing the way of Jesus with their lives and lips. After just one year, the town was transformed: an astounding drop in addiction, significantly less sickness, and plentiful prosperity.

What happened in those villages is the fulfillment of a dream Jesus shared in his Sermon on the Mount. Jesus trains us in a way of life that absolutely alters how we treat other people, the authenticity of our piety, and our use of possessions. Why? Because he believes such conduct can change the world. He knows that a Sermon-on-the-Mount lifestyle can renovate the broken-down world.

There are, of course, other reasons to embrace Sermon-on-the-Mount behaviors. One significant reason relates to the way these deeds impact God. We take up Jesus' way because ultimately it is a primary way by which we "give glory to [our] Father who is in heaven" (Mt. 5:16). Jesus believes this way of life honors God. We pursue better connections with people, a greater piety, and a more appropriate stewardship of possessions because of how these show our love for the Lord our God. We seek a Sermon-on-the-Mount existence for the sake of God.

Yet this is not Jesus' only reason for urging us to adopt his alternative lifestyle. He believes that such a life also gives hope to the world. Sermon-on-the-Mount conduct becomes the salt so desperately needed by a decaying people and the light so longed for by those dwelling in the dark (Mt. 5:13–14). We pursue a better connection with people, a greater piety, and a more appropriate stewardship of possessions because of how these show our love for our neighbor. They are the ways in which God uses us to rebuild and revitalize the lives of all who exist on planet earth. A friend of mine named Randy Harris has frequently said that if just a handful of people committed to living by the Sermon on the Mount, the entire world would be changed.

Here's the big idea: spiritual formation is not merely done for *my* sake. It's not like a diet *I* start or an exercise routine *I* commit to just so that *I* may experience self-improvement. Further, allowing Jesus to rewrite the story of my life so that my narrative and the Sermon on the Mount narrative become one is not undertaken solely to bring honor to the Father in heaven. Spiritual formation is never pursued just for me or just for God. It is also pursued for my neighbor. It is also pursued for the sake of the world. The more transformation we experience in the areas of people, piety, and possessions, the better we function as the salt and light of the earth. Sure, we may enjoy some self-improvement. Yes, we will give glory to God. But we will also become the world-changers we were created to be.

This life Jesus describes in Matthew 5–7 is what I call "the Religion of the Real." This is the genuine and authentic spirituality pursued by true followers of God. The Religion of the Real is one that leads others who see it to praise God. It functions as salt and light in the world.

The Power of a Life Poorly Lived

But there is another way to live—a life Jesus describes in a text that mirrors the Sermon on the Mount. This text is his Sermon of Woes (Mt. 23–25). Here Jesus describes the "Faith of the Frauds." This is a phony and forged spirituality pursued by superficial followers of God. The Faith of the Frauds leads others to question God. It functions as decay and darkness in the world rather than as salt and light.

These two sermons from Jesus stand at opposite ends of a continuum:

- The Religion of the Real is the topic of Jesus' first speech in Matthew. The Faith of the Frauds is the topic of his final speech in Matthew.
- Jesus' Sermon on the Mount starts with statements of approval—how God blesses those who practice this real religion. Jesus' Sermon of Woes starts with statements of disapproval—how God curses those who practice this fraudulent faith. The seven "woes" in Matthew 23 are the antithesis of the eight "blessed are" statements in Matthew 5.

There could be numerous reasons for Jesus' woeful condemnation of the fraudulent followers of God. Jesus could speak volumes about how their hypocrisy is hurting themselves, how it leads to a lack of self-fulfillment. He could also preach endlessly about the way in which their pretense offends God. God is wounded and weary from their superficiality.

But one of the primary reasons Jesus slams this superficial way of life is due to the negative impact the Faith of the Frauds has on the world. For example, Jesus reports that the insincerity and duplicity of the scribes and Pharisees is slamming the door of the kingdom of God in the faces of people trying to get in, and is leading people straight to hell (Mt. 23:13–15). The world is actually worse off because of the presence of hypocritical religious people. In contrast, those who practice the Religion of the Real have a positive impact on the world (Mt. 5).

Contemporary commentators agree. Theologian Karl Rahner writes, "The number one cause of atheism is Christians. Those who proclaim God with their mouths and deny Him with their lifestyles is what an unbelieving world finds simply unbelievable."[13] Rahner is describing the Faith of the Frauds: Christians who proclaim God with their mouths while denying him with their lifestyles. And Rahner finds that this faith does exactly what Jesus predicted: it slams shut the door to the kingdom. It causes an unbelieving world to continue disbelieving.

Yet the authentic spirituality Jesus outlines in his Sermon on the Mount is just the opposite. It betters the world. It flavors and enlightens the world. And, for this reason, Jesus commends it.

Spiritual formation is not embraced solely for our own sake or for God's sake. It is also embraced because of its sweeping influence on the world around us.

In February, the *Washington Times* ran a story on Christianity in China.[14] One piece of the article read this way: "Beijing wants to limit the exposure of a religion based on charity, self-sacrifice and love of neighbor. Christians were barred from participating in relief efforts after the April 2010 earthquake in northwest China because the government feared they would set too good an example and attract converts." What Beijing feared might happen is what Jesus guarantees will happen. It's why Jesus blesses the Religion of the Real. People who live it will set such a good example that they will attract converts. It makes the world a better place.

Your Sentence for Their Sake

Jesus thus changes the whole tone of spiritual formation. It's not just about *my* private spiritual fulfillment. It's not merely about *my* personal relationship with him. It's now also about my contribution to the kingdom. It's about my playing a role in the greater story of God to renew and recreate the earth and all its people. As I experience greater degrees of divine transformation, I become better able to fulfill my purpose of blessing all people. Jesus wants me to grow in these key areas of piety, people, and possessions—for my sake and his sake and the world's sake.

TAKE ⑩

How, then, might you rewrite the sentences of your life? Take ten minutes today to amend the sentences you jotted down in chapter 2. This time, craft the sentences with the rest of the world in mind.

For the sake of the world, God, help my connection with people to be _____.

For the sake of the world, God, help my walk with you to be

_____.

For the sake of the world, God, help my use of possessions to be

_____.

4

Four Principles of Life Change

Saying Goodbye to Air Hockey

While my family and I recently gorged on the feast of adventure and fun at Disney World and Universal Studios, we paused one afternoon for our stomachs to enjoy some lunch at an indoor shop. Near our table, a five-or-six-year-old child was passionately playing an air hockey game. When the game ended, his father beckoned him so they could return to the amazing attractions outside. But the son refused. "I want to play this game again!" he whined. "I want to play air hockey!" he protested. Some of the most creative, unique, and awe-inspiring rides awaited him just outside that door. But all he could focus on was a tired old game that floats a plastic disc on a bed of air.

Sometimes I'm like that boy. I focus on things that, in the big picture, are ordinary and common. Things unlikely to lead to any measure of true fulfillment. I focus on a life that is average and run-of-the-mill. But then Jesus beckons me, beckons us, out to the most thrilling and uncommon life ever imagined. Through his Sermon on the Mount, he invites us to experience a unique, creative, and transforming life with God, with others, and with possessions. He paints a vision of life that makes the one we're living look as feeble as the life of a boy who won't leave his air hockey for the world's greatest attractions. And if I'd just take Jesus' hand, he'd lead me into a *truly* magic kingdom.

But how does his vision become a reality? How do we put down the plastic paddle and walk with Jesus into this exceptional and matchless life?

One way to answer these questions is to look at and listen to one who already made this transition. The apostle Paul was one such person. Once upon a time, Paul chose a life that was selfish, arrogant, violent, intolerant, judgmental, and impatient. His eyes were blind to the fact that this way of existing fell sadly and immeasurably short of the one for which God had created him. But the day came when Paul, in awe, dropped the plastic paddles. Jesus granted him a view of an alternative life that was so gloriously different it literally blinded him. Paul took Jesus' hand and walked into a new life of generosity, humility, gentleness, hospitality, acceptance, and patience. He embarked on an uncommon and world-changing adventure. Every minute of his schedule and each task on his list were shaped by Jesus' Sermon-on-the-Mount ethic.

Writing to Christians in Philippi, Paul shares some of the details behind his epic transformation. He reveals in broad strokes what led him from one life to the other:

> But whatever gain I had, I counted as loss for the sake of Christ. Indeed, I count everything as loss because of the surpassing worth of knowing Christ Jesus my Lord. For his sake I have suffered the loss of all things and count them as rubbish, in order that I may gain Christ and be found in him, not having a righteousness of my own that comes from the law, but that which comes through faith in Christ, the righteousness from God that depends on faith—that I may know him and the power of his resurrection, and may share his sufferings, becoming like him in his death, that by any means possible I may attain the resurrection from the dead. Not that I have already obtained this or am already perfect, but I press on to make it my own, because Christ Jesus has made me his own. Brothers, I do not consider that I have made it my own. But one thing I do: forgetting what lies behind and straining forward to what lies ahead, I press on toward the goal for the prize of the upward call of God in Christ Jesus. Let those of us who are mature think this way, and if in anything you think otherwise, God will reveal that also to you. Only let us hold true to what we have attained. Brothers, join in imitating me, and keep your eyes on those who walk according to the example you have in us. (Phil. 3:7–17)

Paul points to at least four general principles that allowed him to take Jesus' hand and leave the air hockey behind. He testifies to at least four wide-ranging truths that are necessary if we too wish to start living into Jesus' Sermon-on-the-Mount life. Contemporary authors such as

Richard Foster, Dallas Willard, John Ortberg, Marjorie Thompson, Jan Johnson, Tony Jones, Mark Buchanan, and Henri Nouwen have helped me to identify and name these principles.

End Over Errors

As I've walked with people along this journey into Jesus' way of life, I've noticed that many struggle with a fundamental issue. When they fall and fail (and they frequently do), people tend to get down and discouraged. They can't stop thinking about how, once again, they've fallen short of the life for which they were created. And they begin to think that such a life is only a fairy tale; it's a story whose happy ending they'll never quite reach. They get engrossed in how many times they lost their temper that month, how many mornings they didn't pray that week, or how many people they didn't serve that day. It doesn't matter how many spiritual successes they experienced that month, week, or day. All they can see are the failures. They forget the hits. They forget the runs. All they notice are the errors.

This battle was once my friend Alice's worst fight. We meet monthly for prayer and spiritual coaching. When we began years ago, Alice could only talk about her spiritual errors. How she let an unkind word slip again. How she began another day without prayer. The more she talked, the more she despaired. But then we began to explore Paul's testimony. And one particular line stuck out: "But one thing I do: forgetting what lies behind and straining forward to what lies ahead, I press on toward the goal…" Even Paul admits, "Not that I have already obtained this or am already perfect." Even Paul still made errors. But those errors were not his focus. Instead, his eyes remained glued on the end, the goal, the vision of life he found in Jesus Christ. When Paul failed to achieve that vision, he put that mistake in the past and kept his focus on the goal. He oriented his life toward forgetting what was behind–the failures and the falls–and kept straining and pressing on toward the goal–the unique and exemplary life modeled for us by Jesus. Alice memorized Paul's line. Every time she starts to dwell in our sessions on some flaw, she almost immediately quotes Paul's words: "But, I'm going to forget what lies behind and strain toward what lies ahead." These days she and I spend a lot less time talking about errors and a lot more time talking about the end–the goal toward which she is striving.

Leadership experts Warren Bennis and Burt Nanus have famously observed, "[P]eople move in the direction of their most dominant thought."[15] Applied to spiritual growth, this principal postulates that if all you think about is your character failures, or your lack of Bible reading, or how you misspent your money, you may actually keep moving in that direction. You may just keep repeating the same mistakes. However, if you focus instead on a compelling and positive vision for what your life could be, you will move in *that* direction.

I'm not suggesting it's wrong to recognize and acknowledge our errors. Some of the most fruitful spiritual disciplines are those like the *Examen* (discussed later), which are designed to open our eyes to some of our most glaring weaknesses. The challenge many of us face, however, is a tendency to think only or primarily of those weaknesses. We stare so long at the darkness of our errors that eventually we become blind to anything else. Those who make real progress in any facet of life—athletics, business, or spiritual growth—acknowledge their shortcomings but are not handicapped by them.

As I've noted earlier, Dallas Willard writes that lasting change in life takes place in three steps summarized by the letters V, I, M. First, we embrace a *Vision* of the kind of life into which we wish to move. Second, we make an *Intentional* decision that we're going to pursue that vision. Third, we determine the *Means* for living out that vision. The process always begins with vision and is sustained by vision. I believe this is what Paul reveals from his own life. He freely admitted his errors, but those errors did not take up residence in his mind. The primary occupant of his mind was Jesus' vision for life. Paul forgot what was behind; he left the past in the past. And he just kept straining and striving toward what was ahead. We would do well to do the same.

Effort Over Earning

Some who are enamored with Jesus' Sermon-on-the-Mount life and who reach the moment in their lives when they wish to genuinely start living that life find themselves paralyzed by an inability to differentiate effort from earning. It dawns on them that a transition from the run-of-the-mill life they are living to the over-the-top life Jesus offers will require intense effort. They grasp that climbing from passion to purity, from fury to forgiveness, and from greed to generosity necessitates nearly superhero levels of strength. Yet they've drunk so deeply of Scripture's teaching about grace as unmerited favor that "effort" sounds very much like "earn." And they are not about to return to the demanding and discouraging life of somehow trying to earn their way into God's way of life. Thus they are caught between a dream to experience the mountaintop life of Jesus and a dread that any work toward that mountaintop will just lead them back to legalism.

Paul's crystal clear awareness of this issue leads him to write of "not having a righteousness of my own that comes from the law, but that which comes through faith in Christ, the righteousness from God that depends on faith." Paul's transformation from intolerance to inclusiveness and from hatred to hospitality, and the effort associated with it, wasn't even a distant cousin twice removed to "a righteousness...that comes from the law." There was no relationship at all between the two. When Paul encountered the risen Jesus on his way to the city of Damascus, he was forced to drop everything— especially the baggage of legalism and works righteousness that formed the core of spirituality at that time. Paul no longer believed it possible or necessary to earn God's favor or win his righteousness. He leaves no doubt on this issue. His own spiritual renovation had absolutely nothing to do with earning or winning. Paul wants us to know that we've all been freely given a right standing with God, and no amount of spiritual renovation is going to make God love us more.

But while God is opposed to earning, as Dallas Willard writes, he is not opposed to effort. Twice in the testimony above, Paul writes about how he "presses on," and once he describes how he is "straining forward." This is the language of effort. Intense effort. Sweat-dropping-from-your-head effort. And effort is not the same as earning.

Here is how Dallas Willard explains it:

> While it is true that we are saved by grace, that God alone is the author of our salvation, and it is impossible to change our wayward hearts on our own, it is also true that we have important responsibilities in this journey of discipleship. We must understand the critical truth that God is not opposed to people making an effort, but that God is opposed to using our effort to earn salvation. So God is not opposed to effort but to earning. While God's grace birthed us into the kingdom, our continued cooperation with that grace grows us in the life of the kingdom.[16]

God is opposed to earning—that posture that proposes: "I can save myself." But God is not opposed to effort—the actions we undertake to become more and more spiritually healthy. And if we want to experience more than superficial improvements in our piety, people, and possessions, it will require our intense effort.

But this effort is done in partnership with God. John Ortberg uses a raft, a rowboat, and a sailboat to illustrate this.[17] Imagine that the shoreline on the opposite side of a lake represents where you dream of living. That shore is you experiencing Matthew 5–7 every single day. How do you get to that shore? You could jump onto a raft and assume that God's going to do all the work for you, but you'd just end up drifting aimlessly. Alternatively, you could jump into a rowboat and assume that you alone must do all the work. So you row and row, but eventually you burn out. What you need is a sailboat. Sailing is not easy. It still requires intense effort. But, ultimately, the wind carries you to the other shore. You and the wind co-labor. In the same way, you and God will co-labor to achieve true life-change.

Compass Over Clock[18]

The more I've talked with people striving to let Jesus' Sermon on the Mount shape their to-do's, time, and targets, the more I've found that we too regularly watch the clock and too rarely consider the compass. This tendency hamstrings our journey toward spiritual transformation.

Which is your tendency—to watch the clock or consider the compass? Reflect on the questions you ask yourself about spiritual growth. You are watching the clock when the primary questions asked about life-change are these: "How fast am I growing?" "How quickly am I changing?" "How soon will I arrive at spiritual maturity?" What matters most to those of us who watch the clock is haste and hustle: getting there with haste; showing lots of hustle.

Alternatively, you are considering the compass when these questions fill your mind: "Am I headed in the right direction?" "Am I making progress?" "Am I pointing at the right goals?" What matters most to those of us who consider the compass is trend and trajectory: trending in the right direction; travelling on the right trajectory.

One of the primary sources of discouragement in the spiritual journey stems from the clock. We despair because we're not growing in prayer promptly enough or becoming a servant swiftly enough or overcoming rage rapidly enough. We are clock watchers. And clock watching inevitably leads to disappointment because none of us develops as quickly as we desire.

Thankfully, the issue Paul models in his testimony to the Philippians is not accomplishment but aim. His ultimate concern is not rapidity ("Am moving at the right speed?") but route ("Am I moving in the right direction?"). When it came to Paul's own transformation, he did not watch the clock. Instead, he considered the compass.

We know this by listening closely to the confession he makes in his statement to the Philippians. By the time Paul writes to the followers of Jesus in Philippi, he has followed Jesus for about thirty years. Yet despite devoting himself to the Christ-curriculum for three decades, Paul is far from graduation. He explains:

> Not that I have already obtained this or am already perfect, but I press on to make it my own, because Christ Jesus has made me his own. Brothers, I do not consider that I have made it my own. But one thing I do: forgetting what lies behind and straining forward to what lies ahead, I press on toward the goal for the prize of the upward call of God in Christ Jesus. (Phil. 3:12–14)

Paul is transparent: "I haven't obtained Christ-likeness. I am not yet perfect. I've not made Jesus' teaching fully my own." Even after thirty years Paul freely admits to falling short of the vision Jesus has for his character and his conduct. "If I were a clock-watcher," Paul is acknowledging, "I'd have given up. I'd have quit for my lack of quickness. My forward movement has been too snaillike to suit a clock-watcher."

But the discrepancy between where he is and where he wants to be does not discourage him. Why? Because he is concentrating, not on the clock, but on the compass. Paul strains toward *what is ahead.* He presses on toward *the goal.* What matters is being on the correct course, not having an acceptable acceleration. What counts is the target before him, not the ground behind him. Paul does not fret about how fast he is growing. Instead, he focuses on the fact that he *is* growing—gradually and on an accurate bearing.

Our culture is oriented around quick and easy. We want to overcome anger in one week. We want to become more kind in ten days. We desire spiritual triumph in as little time as possible. But true life-renovation is neither quick nor easy. It is slow and steady. What matters is the compass. Are we moving in the right direction, slowly and steadily?

Malcolm Gladwell quotes neurologist Daniel Levitin in his book *Outliers* on what it takes to become an expert: "The emerging picture from such studies is that ten thousand hours of practice is required to achieve the level of mastery associated with being a world-class expert—in anything… In study after study, of composers, basketball players, fiction writers, ice skaters, concert pianists, chess players, master criminals and what have you, this number comes up again and again…"[19] Ten thousand hours is the time required to achieve mastery in any area of life. Ten thousand hours. Perhaps what is true for the pianist is true regarding purity. Perhaps what is necessary for composers is true regarding compassion. Mastering the character and conduct of the Sermon on the Mount just may require ten thousand hours.

Want to become a master at prayer? Invest ten thousand hours of practice. Wish to rise to the level of an elite giver? Put in the required ten thousand hours of rehearsal. This means if you pray one hour a day, it may take twenty-seven years to attain the perfect prayer. If you labor thirty minutes a day on generosity, it may take fifty-four years before it's instinctual and natural.

The expedition from the foothills where you now reside to the summit to which Jesus points is one of ten thousand steps. This passage is not a sprint; it is a marathon. It is not a day's walk; it is a life's project. So tuck the clock away deep into your pack. Its *tick-tick-tick* will only become a source of dangerous irritation. Like the pebble in your hiking book, it will eventually rub your spirit and soul raw. Instead, keep your eye on the compass. When you wander off course, let the compass guide you back. Don't look behind to see how much territory you've traversed. Just look ahead to the summit. Keep your eye there.

Training Over Trying

There is one final fundamental key to laying down the air hockey and following Jesus out the door to his larger-than-life-sized plan: focus on training harder rather than trying harder. Dallas Willard writes, "As disciples, we are not *trying* to be different people (which is the road to failure, legalism, and bondage), but we are *training* to be different people."[20] You will not become victorious over vice by just trying harder. You will not subdue sin merely through brute force. As you peer up the slopes of Jesus' Sermon on the Mount, do not think, "If I just push myself really hard, I'll make it to the top."

Effort *is* required. But no significant spiritual growth takes place through effort alone. The effort must be expended in the right way. What's called for is not trying harder, but training harder. John Ortberg succinctly states, "Respecting the distinction between training and merely trying is the key to transformation in every aspect of life."[21]

Most of us have accepted this truth in the realm of physical fitness. I have a group of friends who regularly run the half-marathon or full marathon in Memphis. The event serves as a fundraiser for Saint Jude Children's Research Hospital. Many of these friends have run the race multiple times. And each year they enter into a familiar rhythm. Months prior to the event they begin training. While they may have been actively running throughout the year, in order to prepare for the

Saint Jude half- or full marathon, they know they must do something different. They must train.

Slowly, methodically, over a period of months, they run longer distances and log greater numbers of miles. At training's beginning, their "long run" may be only eight miles. Two weeks later it's ten miles. Not long after that the "long run" progresses to twelve miles. Through the training, they are able to gradually build up their endurance, strength, and capacity for discomfort. When race day arrives, they are again able to do what they could not do just a few months earlier—run 13.1 or 26.2 miles.

Once in a while, a friend will try to bypass training. A few years ago after the half-marathon, I exited the baseball stadium where the race finishes and began walking to my car. I saw one of my running friends sitting on some steps near the stadium's entrance. She was pale, sweaty, and breathing hard. "What's wrong?" I asked. The race had completed over an hour ago. Her body should have recovered by now. She confessed, "I didn't make time to train this year. I only had a handful of long runs and figured I could just push myself to the finish line this year. Boy, was that a mistake!" She didn't train hard in the months prior to the race and instead just tried hard on the day of the race. It left her body such a wreck she vowed never to do that again.

In his Sermon on the Mount, Jesus is showing us the entire race. It's not a 5K. It's a marathon. Complete the 26.2-mile race and this is what your life will look like. But this race is not something we can complete in our present state of spiritual fitness. We must humbly accept that none of us possess the spiritual muscle and stamina to successfully cross that finish line. Instead, we must enter into training. We must discover ways to slowly, methodically, and intentionally build up our spiritual muscles over time.

This is precisely the purpose of the spiritual disciplines found in the remainder of this book. Engage in them and eventually, through the empowerment of the Holy Spirit, you will become capable of doing what you may have never been able to do before. You will find yourself living into this amazing vision Jesus has for your life.

Paul points to this progressive growth when he urges the Philippians to "work out your own salvation with fear and trembling, for it is God who works in you, both to will and to work for his good pleasure" (Phil. 2:12b–13). We do not work *for* our salvation. But we do *work out* our salvation, partnering with the God who gives us both the desire (will) and ability (work) to live "for his good pleasure." Spiritual training is how we work out the saving work of God within us.

TAKE ⑩

Here are the principles to remember and act on:

1. Keep in mind the end in front of you instead of the errors behind you.
2. Focus on expending great effort for God, not on earning something from God.
3. Consider the compass rather than watching the clock.
4. Dedicate yourself to strategically training harder, rather than simply trying harder.

Which of these principles do you most need to embrace? Take ten minutes to reflect on that question. Specifically, take ten to prayerfully consider your responses to the lines below:

To better grow in piety (my relationship with God), people (my relationship with others), or possessions (my relationship with material goods), I need to prioritize principle #_____.

One way I've struggled with this principle is

_____.

One way I can do better living by this principle is:

_____.

SECTION TWO

Genuine in Piety

5

Swimming beyond the Shallow End

In the first section of this book, we firmly impressed on our hearts and minds Jesus' dream for life. His is a comprehensive concept that involves living rightly with God (piety), with others (people), and with money and material things (possessions). We laid aside all other portraits of our purpose and embraced Jesus' portrait.

In sections 2 through 4, we will learn and practice twelve spiritual disciplines I have selected because of their ability to help us better live out the Sermon on the Mount. section 1 laid out the vision. Sections 2 through 4 focus on the means. The twelve spiritual habits are the means by which we enter into training so that we can experience Holy-Spirit-powered growth in piety, people, and possessions. And, true to this book's title, each of these disciplines can be practiced in ten minutes or less.

In section 2 we will emphasize growing in piety. Our aim is to use four spiritual disciplines to undergo transformation in our most important relationship—with God. To give ourselves and our God plenty of time to nurture this growth, we will spend three days observing each spiritual habit before moving on to the next one. Enjoy these next twelve days. They just may be the most rewarding days you've spent in a long time.

Increasing Depth

Though I read them for the first time many years ago, the opening lines in Richard Foster's classic on spiritual development refuse to untangle themselves from the web of my mind: "Superficiality is the curse of our age... The desperate need today is not for a greater number of intelligent people, or gifted people, but for deep people."[1] In important ways, this is a summary of Jesus' compelling call. He invites us out of a life of spiritual superficiality and into one of spiritual depth. He demands we exchange a spirituality of inches for one without measure.

This theme takes center stage in Jesus' teaching on piety in the Sermon on the Mount (Mt. 6:1–18) and again in his follow-up sermon in Matthew 23. Three times in Matthew 6:1–18 Jesus warns against practicing piety before others for their applause. Seven times in Matthew 23 he warns against masquerading as spiritual people in order to gain respect and status. In Matthew 6:1–18 he calls for a piety that is practiced in private rather than performed for the public, while in Matthew 23 he demands a spirituality that doesn't just look attractive on our outside but also labors aggressively on our inside.

One spiritual practice uniquely suited to moving beyond the superficial in our walk with the Father is the *Examen.* The *Examen* was introduced by Ignatius Loyola in the 1500s.

Ignatius Loyola

Born in 1491, Loyola was one of thirteen children in a family of minor nobility in northern Spain. As a youngster, Loyola was inspired by the ideals of knighthood. He daydreamed of doing epic and heroic deeds. Then, in 1521, while fighting in a battle against the French, Loyola was gravely wounded. During a long recovery, he filled the time reading about the life of Jesus and about the lives of those who followed Jesus. These stories deeply affected Loyola. He no longer simply dreamed of doing heroic deeds. He dreamed of doing heroic deeds–for God. He was stirred by the examples of holy ones, such as Francis of Assisi, who abandoned themselves wholly to God. After healing from his wounds, Loyola determined to follow the steps of the most devout believers in Jesus. He would practice a radical and deep form of discipleship.

Loyola recruited a small group with similar visions–people unsatisfied with the shallow or superficial regarding their spirituality. Together they formed the Society of Jesus, also known as the Jesuits. And to fuel a faith that would be intense and all-consuming, the Jesuits embraced two core practices. Loyola believed the Holy Spirit could use these two disciplines to bring substantial depth to their spirituality. These were the Spiritual Exercises and the *Examen.*

Through research of spiritual masters and through his own trial-and-error experiences in coaching others in spiritual growth, Loyola began collecting the best-of-the-best prayers, meditations, and spiritual practices. He combined these into the Spiritual Exercises. He then crafted a thirty-day retreat during which people interested in substantial spiritual growth would experience these exercises. It was a "boot camp" designed to deepen one's piety.

The second core practice of the Jesus Society was the *Examen.* If the Spiritual Exercises were the booster rockets designed to get piety off the launch pad, the *Examen* was the ongoing source of fuel needed to propel faith day by day. The *Examen* was a structured form of prayer that Loyola urged people to practice at least twice daily.

The *Examen* consists of five steps. For simplicity's sake, I've reduced their number to four, and rewritten their titles. In this way they are more easily memorized and internalized. You can progress through the four phases in about ten minutes. Conducted twice a day (e.g., noon and nighttime), the *Examen* will intensify and deepen your connection to Christ and the Father.

Step 1: Recognize (the presence of God)

The first step in the *Examen* is to recognize that you are in the presence of God. While we are always in God's presence, the *Examen* begins with an intentional remembering that God is present at this very moment. Frankly, during a typical day we often forget God. The *Examen* is a systematic way to bring God back to mind at key moments.

This first step is an attempt to embrace the reality of the following passages:

- "Where shall I go from your Spirit? / Or where shall I flee from your presence?" (Ps. 139:7)
- "And behold, I am with you always, to the end of the age." (Mt. 28:20b)
- "And he made from one man every nation of mankind to live on all the face of the earth, having determined allotted periods and the boundaries of their dwelling place, that they should seek God, perhaps feel their way toward him and find him. Yet he is actually not far from each one of us, for 'In him we live and move and have our being.'" (Acts 17:26–28a)
- "Keep your life free from love of money, and be content with what you have, for he has said, 'I will never leave you nor forsake you.'" (Heb. 13:5)

The first step in the *Examen* is to recognize the presence of God. This might be done by spending a few moments in silence or by reading a few texts, such as the ones above, or by praying for God to help you know that he is with you right now.

Step 2: Request (enlightenment from God)

In the second step we request enlightenment from God and his Spirit. Specifically, we ask God to fill us with wisdom and discernment as we move into the next step of the *Examen*. There, we will be reviewing a portion of our day. We wish to conduct this review with an eyesight and insight only God can grant. Knowing that in our weaknesses we are likely to miss something God wishes us to see, we now request that God, through his Spirit, opens our eyes and hearts.

In step 2, we are putting the following promises to the test:

- "If any of you lacks wisdom, let him ask God, who gives generously to all without reproach, and it will be given him." (Jas. 1:5)
- "Ask, and it will be given to you; seek, and you will find; knock, and it will be opened to you. For everyone who asks receives, and the one who seeks finds, and to the one who knocks it will be opened." (Mt. 7:7–8)

Before we begin the journey of reviewing our day, we implore God to illuminate the way.

Step 3: Review (the day's highs and lows with God)

In the third step of the *Examen,* we review the past day or half-day with God. Like an athlete and coach watching a video from a recent contest, we and God watch the past few hours of our day as they are projected on the screen of our minds. At various points, we pause the video to stare more closely at an event, or rewind a segment in order to see something we may have missed. As we gaze, we ask questions and take mental notes.

This review is not driven by a dry interest in chronology, as if all we were interested in was a timeline of the day's events. It is fueled by an interest in theology, spirituality, and morality. We are striving to assess not just what happened in the past day or half-day. We are hoping to gain insight into emotions and motives that drove our behaviors and what God was up to in the midst of these behaviors. We are hoping to observe divine patterns or human habits that teach us something about ourselves and our God. More specifically, we are seeking to identify situations that reveal both positive and negative things to us. We want to mark the triumphs and the tragedies of the past hours, paying special attention to how God was present in both.

There is much flexibility regarding how we perform this review. Adele Calhoun's six questions, however, may provide a helpful structure.[2] We might choose one or two of these questions to ponder as we rehearse the past day or half-day:

1. For what moment today am I most grateful? For what moment today am I least grateful?
2. When did I give and receive the most love today? When did I give and receive the least love today?
3. What was the most life-giving part of my day? What was the most life-thwarting part of my day?
4. When today did I have the deepest sense of connection with God, others, and myself? When today did I have the least sense of connection?
5. Where was I aware of living out the fruit of the Spirit? Where was there an absence of the fruit of the Spirit?
6. Where did I experience desolation? Where did I find consolation?

Ultimately, we are endeavoring to become more conscious of the ways in which God showed up during our day and how we helped or hindered his activity. These questions enlighten us as to how God is moving in our day. They help us learn what he may be saying to us through the routine of ordinary events.

It is vital to attend to both the high points and the low points when practicing the *Examen*. Those of us who habitually remember only bad things will be empowered to remember that the day was also filled with good things. And those of us who regularly only recall the good moments will be challenged to wrestle with the reality of the day's bad moments.

Step 4: Resolve (to live for God)

In the final step, we move from pondering over the past to planning for the future. Having reviewed the highs and lows of the past day or half-day, we now consider the half-day or full day in front of us. We prayerfully ask, "What is God teaching me through this review that will impact the way I live in the next half-day or full day?" If the *Examen* has revealed some sinful habits, we now consider how to address those habits in the hours before us. If the *Examen* has brought to mind some recent blessings of God, we now ask how we might live in gratitude and praise during the moments ahead. Based on the review, are there relationships to mend? Are there sins to repent of? Are there tasks that need doing? As we leave the *Examen*, we resolve to live the next day or half-day in light of what we've learned from the past day or half-day.

TAKE ⑩

Let's take ten minutes right now and practice the *Examen*. For practice, let's just consider the last half-day.

Recognize

Close your eyes. Breathe in and out, slowly. Repeat these words to yourself silently: "You are with me always. You will never leave me nor forsake me." Recognize that God is present right here and right now.

Request

Quietly ask God to fill you with wisdom and discernment. Repeat this prayer: "God, give me eyes to see what you see. Fill me with insight and illumination as I review this last half-day."

Review

Lead your mind back several hours and begin to play forward the events as they happened, right up to the present moment. While there are many highs and lows to consider, for practice consider your answer to just these two questions: When today did I have the deepest sense of connection with God, others, and myself? When today did I have the least sense of connection? Review the past few hours with just these two questions in mind.

Resolve

Having identified a time of deep connection and a time of superficial connection during the past few hours, now answer this question: What is God saying to me through this review? What do I resolve to do as a result of this review? Is there a relationship to nurture or repair? Is there a work of my flesh to repent of? Is there an issue to lift to God in prayer? Is there a task or project that needs to become a priority? What does God wish me to do based on my review of the past half-day?

6

Unforgetting God

I once heard Dallas Willard at a California congregation. He was speaking about how intolerable times of pain may become unexpected times of praise when we experience the presence of God within them. Willard said, "Experiencing the presence of God in one's life is something you've got to have before you need it, like water before a fire." If you wait for a fire to spark before you secure water, you're too late. In the same way, if you wait for pain to hit before you cultivate an ongoing sense of the presence of God in your life, you're too late. Willard stressed that we must constantly "practice the presence of God." Throughout each day we must cultivate a conviction that God is with us. Then, when we meet moments that suggest God is gone, our past experience with God will overcome our present doubts about him.

But how do we do this? How do we nurture a constant sense of the companionship of God? A recent conversation in a church hallway with four friends focused on this question. Cary told of an overseas flight he took to Ukraine. Hours into the trip, he left his seat and walked the aisles to stretch his legs. Eventually he bumped into a man who was stretching his soul. The man, clasping a small prayer rug, was seeking solitude on the airplane to engage in "*salat*." Like one-and-a-half billion Muslims worldwide, this traveler was dedicated to praying five times each day. Even on an international flight, he was trying to tend to this prayerful practice. While *salat* serves many purposes, above all it reminds the one praying that God is near. In a CNN profile, one man shared: "It reminds you about God throughout your day. At fixed intervals, no matter how busy you are, all of a sudden you have to take out a few minutes and you're remembering,

OK, why am I really here?"[3] After Cary shared this story, my friend Joe remarked, "I need something like that. When I'm working, it's hard for me to think about anything but work. I need something to remind me of God throughout the day."

I'm a lot like Joe. You may be too. We often forget God during the day. We need a way to unforget God—some technique to turn our minds back to God when our thoughts have wandered from him. Some method, as Brother Lawrence counseled, to "Forget him the very least you can."[4]

The *Examen* provides this and more. It creates a structure through which we are not only reminded of God through the day, but we are guided, in specific ways, to interact deeply and significantly with God throughout the day. Whether it is practiced twice a day (e.g., morning and noon), or three times a day (e.g., morning, noon, and evening), the *Examen* pauses all other activity and invites us to enjoy God's company.

Audience of One

A fixed focus on the persistent presence of God is central to the piety Jesus speaks of in the Sermon on the Mount. Jesus introduces his message on spirituality in Matthew 6 by urging us to consider our audience. Too many of us, Jesus warns, think only of "other people in order to be seen by them" rather than concentrating on our "Father who is in heaven" (Mt. 6:1). Throughout his message, Jesus contrasts this divine audience of one with the human audience of many whom some seek to impress with inflated acts of piety. God, Jesus teaches, is always close and is the only spectator with whom we should be concerned.

Thus, when we "give to the needy" that we might honor the Almighty, we recognize our "Father who sees in secret" (Mt. 6:4). When we pray on our knees that we might commune with our Creator, we acknowledge our "Father who sees in secret" (6:6). And when we fast from food that we might feast on the Father, we believe in the attendance of a "Father who sees in secret" (6:18).

Jesus speaks often in his presentation on piety about the "reward" of spirituality (Mt. 6:1, 2, 4, 5, 6, 16, 18). He suggests that piety is at its most rewarding when we experience God as a constant companion. Even when we are "in secret" (or, *especially* when we are "in secret"), the Father is present and aware of all we are and do. He never forgets us. He is never oblivious of us. But we miss the reward of Jesus' religion because we miss this basic truth. *We* forget God. *We* become oblivious of him. And our attention falls on the audience of many rather than the audience of one. But Jesus calls us back to a devotion grounded in the soil of this straightforward fact: God is at hand.

The *Examen* is an easy way to live into this reality. It is a means by which we can experience the companionship of God throughout the day. Twice or three times a day we pause all activity and attend to God.

TAKE ⑩

Spiritual director and author David Fleming provides a wonderfully simple translation of the *Examen*.[5] Take ten minutes right now and use it to fall back into the arms of the One who's never left your side.

God, thank you.

I thank you, God, for always being with me, but especially I am grateful that you are with me right now.

God, send your Holy Spirit upon me.

God, let the Holy Spirit enlighten my mind and warm my heart that I may know where and how we have been together this day.

God, let me look at my day.

God, where have I felt your presence, seen your face, heard your word this day? God, where have I ignored you, run from you, perhaps even rejected you this day?

God, let me be grateful and ask forgiveness.

God, I thank you for the times this day we have been together and worked together. God, I am sorry for the ways that I have offended you by what I have done or what I did not do.

God, stay close.

God, I ask that you draw me ever closer to you this day and tomorrow. God, you are the God of my life—thank you.

7

Identifying Your
Invisible Iniquity

At Seattle's Boeing Field, brand new commercial jets are put through their paces.[6] During test flights in 2004, Boeing discovered serious problems in several new planes. Mechanics found glass beads destroying the inside of the engines. The beads, about the size of sugar granules, wrecked the engines beyond repair. Officials set out to determine the source of the beads. Eventually, their investigation led them to a runway. New reflective lines had just been painted on the airstrip. The paint contained small glass beads that reflected light. But the paint was defective. On one patch of paint, the granules were separating from the paint. As the plane engines increased thrust and passed this patch, they sucked up these granules. The result was fifty million dollars of damage.

Sometimes it is the tiny threats that cause some of the greatest harm. This is especially true in our spiritual life. In his Sermon on the Mount, Jesus identifies spiritual roadblocks that seemed invisible to even the most devout in his day. The mystical masters of Jesus' world could certainly spot spiritual roadblocks such as murder (Mt. 6:21) or adultery (Mt. 6:27). They perceived with precision that immoralities like these kept people from intimacy with God. But they failed to recognize the spiritual barrier of anger, which was the first step toward murder (Mt. 6:22). They could not detect the barricade of lust, which eventually fueled adultery (Mt. 6:28). In their minds, these were insignificant granules incapable of significant destruction. The professionally pious seemed content to rid their paths of obvious obstacles of murder and adultery. But they remained oblivious to "lesser" yet equally damaging depravities such as anger and lust.

This failure marks all of us, including me. Early in my walk with Jesus, I labored to rid my life of the low-hanging fruit of ungodliness. My sexual impurity was easy to spot and became the object of intense repentance and renewal. But once I tackled the noticeable corruptions like sexual impurity, I relaxed. I slowed down. I figured the fight was basically over.

As I grew older in the faith, however, it began to dawn on me that "lesser" yet similarly significant sins were standing between my Father and me. These iniquities disguised themselves and remained in the shadows. They were woven deep into my habits of thinking, my worldview, and my "natural" tendencies. Only with great intentionality could I even fathom them, much less fight them. I'm talking about my deep hunger for approval, my fear of failure, and my drive to control conditions and colleagues. I soon sought a way to better highlight these hidden sins and deal with them in an aggressive manner. The *Examen* provided exactly what I needed.

Making Visible the Invisible

The word *examen* comes from Latin. It refers to the weight indicator on a balance scale and suggests "an accurate assessment of the true situation."[7] The *Examen* provides an assessment of the true situation between God and ourselves. This spiritual practice allows us to see with greater clarity the big and the small that destroy our spiritual lives. It empowers us to see the tiny but terrible things that come between God and us.

Another name for the *Examen* is the "Prayer of *Examen*." Traditionally, the Prayer of *Examen* has two aspects.[8] The first is an "*examen of consciousness*" through which we recognize the ways in which God has been present to us during the day and how we've responded to that presence. We examine how conscious we have been of God and in what ways he may have been speaking to us or reaching out to us during the day. Because our spiritual lives are so often unexamined, these moments of divine consciousness are often invisible to us. The *Examen* makes them visible.

The second aspect of the Prayer of *Examen* is an "*examen of conscience*" through which we recognize the moral and spiritual areas of our character that require refining. Here, through a detailed review of the past few hours, we bring into focus what may ordinarily be out of sight. We notice the "big" and "small" habits and customs that have either helped or hindered our drawing near to God.

Writing about the *examen* of conscience, St. Ignatius of Loyola states, "Let him go over hour by hour, or period by period, commencing at the hour he rose, and continuing up to the hour and instant of the present *examen*, and let him make…as many dots as were the times he has fallen into that particular sin or defect. Then let him resolve anew to amend himself up to the second *Examen* which he will make."[9] In other words, Loyola recommended making a visual tally of the times we have fallen into a particular sin or defect over the course of several hours–then, with God's help, to resolve to live anew for the remainder of the day.

If you choose to spend an *Examen* reflecting on character issues, it may be helpful to think through different categories of sin.[10] For example, you could consider the list of the seven deadly sins: pride, anger, lust, envy, greed, sloth, and gluttony. I have a set of seven statues in my office. Each one represents one of these sins. Staring at them, I can carefully contemplate ways in which I've committed one or more of these sins during the day. Alternatively, you could use the Ten Commandments (Ex. 20). Or you could reflect on lists in Paul's letters in which he contrasts sins to avoid with qualities to pursue (Rom. 12:9–21; 1 Cor. 13:4–8; Gal. 5:16–23; Col. 3:5–14). With these in mind, during your *Examen* you can consider your answers to two questions: In what ways did I struggle with the sins in this list today? In what ways did I experience the positive qualities in this list today?

If, during an *Examen,* you find that a particular sin shows up again and again, you might choose to dig more deeply by asking yourself: *Why* did I do what I did? *What* happened as a result of my sin?[11] Exploring these two questions can help get at some of the profounder issues underlying that particular sin.

Minister and spiritual-life writer Marjorie Thompson advises that when using an *Examen* to focus on character issues, it is important to "put on neither the rose-colored glasses of naïve optimism nor the gray-colored glasses of needless pessimism."[12] That is, some of us are so positive and uncritical that it's difficult for us to discern any character struggles during our day. Others of us are so negative and critical that it's difficult for us to discern any character successes during our day. This is why the *Examen* necessitates an examination of both highs and lows, successes and failures, steps forward and steps backward.

A daily self-examination like this can be difficult. Yet it returns tremendous dividends. Thompson reminds us of three benefits that flow from the *Examen.*[13] First, it leads to greater self-awareness. The more we truly know ourselves, the better able we are to truly know God. Second, it leads to greater honesty about ourselves. We can now let go of pretense and humbly accept ourselves as we are. Finally, it leads to greater compassion. The more clearly we see ourselves, the less likely we are to judge and critique others. Seeing our brokenness helps us identify with the brokenness in others.

TAKE ⑩

Spiritual director and teacher Ruth Haley Barton provides the following as a way of conducting both an *examen* of consciousness and an *examen* of conscience. Take ten minutes today and follow her pattern of prayer:[14]

1. Look back on the events of the past twenty-four hours, asking God to guide you in seeing what he wants you to see.
2. As you reflect on these events, ask God to show you where he was present with you, even though you may not have recognized it at the time.
3. Ask God to show you the places where you are growing and changing. Thank him for evidence of his transforming work.
4. Ask God to show you places where you fell short of Christlikeness. Be careful not to succumb to shame or morbid introspection; instead, simply name your failure honestly, confess it to God, and receive his forgiveness.
5. Finish by thanking God for the day and for his presence in your life.

8

Praying at Different Elevations

I was recently talking to a friend who is a preaching minister. For several months he had faced an immovable impediment in his ministry. One person was frustrating every move he made to pursue the path he believed God wanted his congregation to take. He and other leaders had discerned bold visions for the church's future, but all plans were on pause because of this single stubborn person. My friend tried everything to alleviate the impasse. He sought to reason with the man. Then, he asked his mentors what to say and do. He even sent other church leaders to speak to the individual. But all this work produced no progress.

Finally, one day a colleague from another congregation asked my friend, "Have you fasted and prayed about this? If I were you, that's what I would do. Fast and pray." My friend had not, but that week he began. He decided to spend each Thursday fasting and praying.

Four weeks later, that intractable individual holding everything up and holding everyone hostage took a job offer in another state.

Prayer had been my friend's last resort, though it should have been his first because, in the end, it was his only resort.

Putting Prayer First

Jesus makes a similar case in his Sermon on the Mount. In Matthew 6:1–18 Jesus speaks specifically about piety, about growing more intimate with the Father. Jesus draws attention to three practices of piety: giving, praying, and fasting. Of the three, Jesus shows prayer to be the most indispensable.

First, Jesus spends greater time speaking on prayer than on the other two practices. Giving receives three verses of Jesus' speech, as does fasting. But prayer receives eleven verses. Jesus devotes nearly four times the space to speaking on prayer as he does highlighting either of these other practices.

Second, when we consider that fasting (Mt. 6:16–18) by its very nature centers on prayer, we can see that two-thirds of Jesus' piety presentation contains instruction and inspiration regarding prayer. So of the eighteen verses in this message on spirituality, fourteen concern prayer.

Third, when Jesus speaks of fasting and giving, he identifies mistakes that other *Jewish* spiritual leaders are making. But in his section on supplication, he additionally identifies mistakes that *Gentile* spiritual leaders are making. He is so intent on ensuring that we experience prayer as originally intended that he doubles his efforts to reveal flawed approaches to it. That is, Jesus spends twice as long clarifying wrong approaches to prayer as he does clarifying wrong approaches to giving or to fasting.

Finally, only in the portion on prayer does Jesus give us a "formula." Only here does he spell out in detail exactly how to "do" prayer. It's here we find the "Lord's Prayer." Though never intended as something that must be said word-for-word, its words nonetheless have become the pathway to richer prayer for centuries. Countless Christians have grown more in tune with the Father and more in line with his will through the words of this prayer than any other prayer. No other section in Jesus' piety presentation contains this level of detailed instruction.

If we wish to dive deeper into the spiritual life, prayer must never be our last resort. It must always be our first resort.

Ready-Made Prayers

Jesus' Lord's Prayer in Matthew 6 is one of what spiritual director Mark Thibodeaux calls "ready-made prayers."[15] Ready-made prayers are those someone else has authored for us. Through them, we speak to God using someone else's words. We could call them pre-packaged or pre-owned. But there is nothing superficial or shallow about them. Instead, by praying them, we are led into spiritual places we may have never reached by relying solely on our own prayer words.

These "pre-owned" prayers provide an experience similar to songs. When a husband sings to his wife or a Christian sings to her Father using words scripted by another person, he or she becomes capable of expressing greater depths of facts and feelings than one could without the song. The same is true with ready-made prayers.

Scripture is full of these petitions. In fact, pastor Adele Calhoun writes, "In the early centuries of the church, believers were taught to pray the Scriptures. Since the Bible is divinely inspired, they believed that praying Scripture deeply connected them to the mind and heart of God. Furthermore, as Scripture was repeatedly prayed, it became memorized. This was a wonderful benefit for those who were illiterate. It also meant that memorized Scripture could lead them to pray at any hour of the day or night."[16] For centuries Christians have relied heavily on the ready-made prayers found in Scripture.

We'll explore three sources of these pre-packaged prayers in the Bible: the Psalms, Jesus' prayers, and the prayers and writings of Paul. We'll begin with Psalms.

Praying the Psalms

The Psalms are the original pre-owned prayers. They are supplications and songs used by the people of God for generations. Learning to pray the Psalms may be the simplest yet most significant step you can take toward growth in your relationship with God.

The Psalms fall into three categories: Orientation, Disorientation, and Reorientation.[17] In psalms of *orientation* God is viewed as trustworthy and reliable. Life is happy, and the one praying is grateful for life's stability and predictability. These psalms provide opportunities to pray about some of the most basic things of life that are responsible for the pleasantness of life. Examples include Psalms 19; 104; and 119.

Like psalms of orientation, psalms of *reorientation* are also prayers of praise and thanksgiving. But rather than focusing on the stability and dependability of the life that God has created, reorientation prayers rejoice for a recent way in which God has delivered the author from despair or danger. They offer praise at its highest and loudest. Examples include Psalms 16; 23; 100; and 150.

Psalms of *disorientation* stand in stark contrast to the other two. These are prayers gasped and groaned when life is at its worst. In them, God seems neither reliable nor likeable. Those who are praying lament their situation in life and beg God for a change in their circumstances. These are the most disturbing prayers in the Old Testament. They include Psalms 13; 51; and 69.

I've found it helpful to reclassify these Old Testament prayers as Prayers from the *Plain* (orientation), Prayers from the *Peak* (reorientation), and Prayers from the *Pit* (disorientation).

- Prayers from the *Plain* are those psalms in which life is ordinary and routine and we thank God for the basic things of life that make life so good.

- Prayers from the *Peak* are those psalms in which life is unusually good and we thank God for a specific way in which he has been active in our lives.
- Prayers from the *Pit* are those psalms in which life is hard and horrible and we give voice to our harshest feelings. They are the prayers that are colored primarily by challenge and suffering in life.

Each kind of psalm stretches us to go beyond what we normally experience in prayer. Prayers from the Plain stretch us to pray about issues we may generally overlook or take for granted, such as a beautiful and life-giving earth or the wise and insight-giving Scriptures. Prayers from the Pit stretch us to grieve to God with bold and unapologetic laments that we may have never used before in prayer. And Prayers from the Peak stretch us to praise in ways we may have never done before in prayer, using colorful, creative, and effusive language.

TAKE ⑩

One way to deepen your prayer life is to pray one psalm each day. You can do this in about ten minutes (you may need to divide up the longer psalms). Some of the psalms can be prayed nearly verbatim. For others, you will need to make some revisions, such as changing second-person or third-person language to first-person. In some cases, you may wish to read the entire psalm and then just paraphrase it to God in your own words.

There are two options for praying a psalm daily: pray through the psalter in numerical order, or pray one type of psalm each day (e.g., a Prayer from the Plain on day 1, a Prayer from the Pit on day 2, and a Prayer from the Peak on day 3). We're going to focus on the second option. Here are nine psalms from which to choose for this exercise:

- From the Plain, Psalm 8; 19; or 78.
- From the Pit, Psalm 13; 51; or 77.
- From the Peak, Psalm 16; 95; or 150.

Take ten minutes right now and pray through one psalm.

9

Talking to the Father
Like the Son

"Did I pray that correctly?"

I'm sometimes asked this question by a friend when we meet for prayer. After she completes a brief time of leading our petitions, she occasionally gives voice to this fear: "Did I pray okay?" She worries that she isn't using the right words in the right way. She frets that she doesn't have the right emphasis and the right emotions.

Another friend regularly asks me to pray on his behalf, something I am honored to do. But there are times when he prefaces his request with remarks such as this: "You always pray better than I do. You always know just what to say. I think God's more likely to answer your prayer about this than he is mine." My friend doubts he can produce the kind of plea that will catch God's ear.

People of prayer have long struggled with this perspective. It's an outlook that views God as one who must be persuaded to act. And only precise prayer words will convince this reluctant God to answer affirmatively.

This was a stance taken by many even in Jesus' day. While preaching about piety in Matthew 6:1–18, Jesus warns:

"The world is full of so-called prayer warriors who are prayer-ignorant. They're full of formulas and programs and advice, peddling techniques for getting what you want from God. Don't fall for that nonsense. This is your Father you are dealing with, and he knows better than you what you need. With a God like this loving you, you can pray very simply." (Mt. 6:7–8, *The Message*).

Some ancient mystics believed they needed the right rule, the perfect program, or the most winsome words in order to get what they wanted from God. Only those who could stitch words together into a flawless format could win over God's heart.

Simple Supplication

However, prayer is intended to be much simpler, as philosopher Peter Kreeft explains:

Prayer is easier than we think... We can all do it, even the most sinful, shallow, silly, and stupid of us. You do not have to master some mystical method. You do not have to master a method at all. Can you talk to a friend? Then you can talk to God, for he is your Friend. And that is what prayer is. The single most important piece of advice about prayer is one word: Begin! God makes it easy: just do it![18]

Prayer *is* easier than we think. It doesn't require seamless sentences and faultless phonetics. It can be as natural and unscripted as a conversation with a friend. Jesus' preferred image is that of a dialogue between a child and a parent: "Pray then like this: 'Our Father...'" (Mt. 6:9).

Still, many of us feel the need for help. We realize we don't need perfect prose or sanctified speech, but we're not sure what to say. We feel a bit like Anne of Green Gables, in the movie of the same name. The movie features Anne Shirley, an orphaned child placed in the home of Marilla and Matthew Cuthbert. One evening Marilla and Anne discuss prayer:

"Have you said your prayers?" Marilla asks Anne.

"I never say any prayers," Anne responds.

"What do you mean? Haven't you been taught to say your prayers?"

"Mrs. Hammond told me that God made my hair red on purpose, and I've never cared for him since."

"Well, while you're under my roof you will say your prayers."

"Why, of course. If you want me to. How does one do it?"

"You thank God for his blessings, and then humbly ask him for the things you want."

"I'll do my best. 'Dear gracious heavenly Father, I thank you for everything. As for the things I especially want, they're so numerous it would take a great deal of time to mention them all. So, I'll just mention the two most important: please let me stay at Green Gables; please make me beautiful when I grow up. I remain yours respectfully, Anne Shirley—with an e.' Did I do all right?"

"Yes, if you were addressing a business letter to the catalog store. Get into bed."

"I should have said 'amen' instead of 'yours respectfully.' Think it'll make any difference?"

"I expect God will overlook it–this time. Good night."[19]

We want to embrace the simplicity of prayer promised by Jesus, but we're so often still unsure of what to say, or how to say it.

The Ready-Made Prayers of Jesus

This is why Jesus introduces us to ready-made prayers. Jesus' "Lord's Prayer" in Matthew 6 is one of these–a pre-written prayer ready to be prayed by any follower of Jesus hungry for help on praying. Through supplications such as this, Jesus takes us by the hand and walks us through a conversation with the Father–not to show us the only words that can ever be used, but to reveal to us themes and habits that make for the most fruitful and enriching times of divine discussion.

This "Lord's Prayer" is only one of many ready-made prayers. The Gospels are filled with other petitions Jesus himself spoke. They provide magnificent mentoring regarding prayer. There are at least ten occasions on which the Gospel authors record the actual words Jesus spoke in prayer. In them we find Jesus praying at least three types of prayers.[20]

First, Jesus prayed inward prayers of complaint. Here, Jesus gave voice to the deepest feelings of disappointment. In his inward prayers of complaint he teaches us how to look deep within ourselves and share dark and discouraging feelings with God in prayer. He teaches us how to complain about our pain. Consider these prayers:

- "Then Jesus went with them to a place called Gethsemane, and he said to his disciples, 'Sit here, while I go over there and pray.' And taking with him Peter and the two sons of Zebedee, he began to be sorrowful and troubled. Then he said to them, 'My soul is very sorrowful, even to death; remain here, and watch with me.' And going a little farther he fell on his face and prayed, saying, 'My Father, if it be possible, let this cup pass from me; nevertheless, not as I will, but as you will.' And he came to the disciples and found them sleeping. And he said to Peter, 'So, could you not watch with me one hour? Watch and pray that you may not enter into temptation. The spirit indeed is willing, but the flesh is weak.' Again, for the second time, he went away and prayed, 'My Father, if this cannot pass unless I drink it, your will be done.' And again he came and found them sleeping, for their eyes were heavy. So, leaving them again, he went away and prayed for the third time, saying the same words again. Then he came to the disciples and said to them, 'Sleep and take your rest later on. See, the hour is at hand, and the Son of Man is betrayed into the hands

of sinners. Rise, let us be going; see, my betrayer is at hand.'"
(Mt. 26:36–46)

- "And when the sixth hour had come, there was darkness over
the whole land until the ninth hour. And at the ninth hour
Jesus cried with a loud voice, 'Eloi, Eloi, lema sabachthani?'
which means, 'My God, my God, why have you forsaken me?'"
And some of the bystanders hearing it said, 'Behold, he is
calling Elijah.' And someone ran and filled a sponge with sour
wine, put it on a reed and gave it to him to drink, saying, 'Wait,
let us see whether Elijah will come to take him down.' And
Jesus uttered a loud cry and breathed his last." (Mk. 15:33–37)
- "After this, Jesus, knowing that all was now finished, said (to
fulfill the Scripture), 'I thirst.' A jar full of sour wine stood
there, so they put a sponge full of the sour wine on a hyssop
branch and held it to his mouth." (Jn. 19:28–29)

Second, Jesus prayed upward prayers of confidence. Despite the darkness
and the despair, Jesus was able to pray upwardly with confidence that
God still ruled, still listened, still reigned, and still cared. Through
these upward prayers of confidence, Jesus shows us how to trust God
even in the darkness.

- "In that same hour he rejoiced in the Holy Spirit and said, 'I
thank you, Father, Lord of heaven and earth, that you have
hidden these things from the wise and understanding and
revealed them to little children; yes, Father, for such was your
gracious will.'" (Lk. 10:21)
- "And Jesus lifted up his eyes and said, 'Father, I thank you that
you have heard me. I knew that you always hear me, but I said
this on account of the people standing around, that they may
believe that you sent me.' When he had said these things, he
cried out with a loud voice, 'Lazarus, come out.'" (Jn. 11:41–
43)
- "And Jesus answered them, 'The hour has come for the Son
of Man to be glorified. Truly, truly, I say to you, unless a grain
of wheat falls into the earth and dies, it remains alone; but if
it dies, it bears much fruit. Whoever loves his life loses it, and
whoever hates his life in this world will keep it for eternal life.
If anyone serves me, he must follow me; and where I am, there
will my servant be also. If anyone serves me, the Father will
honor him. Now is my soul troubled. And what shall I say?
"Father, save me from this hour"? But for this purpose I have
come to this hour. Father, glorify your name.' Then a voice

came from heaven: 'I have glorified it, and I will glorify it
again.' The crowd that stood there and heard it said that it had
thundered. Others said, 'An angel has spoken to him.'" (Jn.
12:23–29).

- "When Jesus had received the sour wine, he said, 'It is
  finished,' and he bowed his head and gave up his spirit." (Jn.
  19:30)[21]

- "It was now about the sixth hour, and there was darkness over
  the whole land until the ninth hour, while the sun's light failed.
  And the curtain of the temple was torn in two. Then Jesus,
  calling out with a loud voice, said, 'Father, into your hands I
  commit my spirit!' And having said this he breathed his last."
  (Lk. 23:44–46)

Third, Jesus prayed outward prayers of compassion. Here Jesus looked
outward and prayed for the needs of friends and foes alike. With his
outward prayers of compassion, Jesus instructs us how to passionately
plea for the people around us.

- "When Jesus had spoken these words, he lifted up his eyes
  to heaven, and said, 'Father, the hour has come; glorify your
  Son that the Son may glorify you, since you have given him
  authority over all flesh, to give eternal life to all whom you
  have given him. And this is eternal life, that they know you
  the only true God, and Jesus Christ whom you have sent. I
  glorified you on earth, having accomplished the work that
  you gave me to do. And now, Father, glorify me in your own
  presence with the glory that I had with you before the world
  existed. I have manifested your name to the people whom
  you gave me out of the world. Yours they were, and you gave
  them to me, and they have kept your word. Now they know
  that everything that you have given me is from you. For I
  have given them the words that you gave me, and they have
  received them and have come to know in truth that I came
  from you; and they have believed that you sent me. I am
  praying for them. I am not praying for the world but for those
  whom you have given me, for they are yours. All mine are
  yours, and yours are mine, and I am glorified in them. And
  I am no longer in the world, but they are in the world, and
  I am coming to you. Holy Father, keep them in your name,
  which you have given me, that they may be one, even as we
  are one. While I was with them, I kept them in your name,
  which you have given me. I have guarded them, and not one

of them has been lost except the son of destruction, that the Scripture might be fulfilled. But now I am coming to you, and these things I speak in the world, that they may have my joy fulfilled in themselves. I have given them your word, and the world has hated them because they are not of the world, just as I am not of the world. I do not ask that you take them out of the world, but that you keep them from the evil one. They are not of the world, just as I am not of the world. Sanctify them in the truth; your word is truth. As you sent me into the world, so I have sent them into the world. And for their sake I consecrate myself, that they also may be sanctified in truth. I do not ask for these only, but also for those who will believe in me through their word, that they may all be one, just as you, Father, are in me, and I in you, that they also may be in us, so that the world may believe that you have sent me. The glory that you have given me I have given to them, that they may be one even as we are one, I in them and you in me, that they may become perfectly one, so that the world may know that you sent me and loved them even as you loved me. Father, I desire that they also, whom you have given me, may be with me where I am, to see my glory that you have given me because you loved me before the foundation of the world. O righteous Father, even though the world does not know you, I know you, and these know that you have sent me. I made known to them your name, and I will continue to make it known, that the love with which you have loved me may be in them, and I in them.'" (Jn. 17:1–26)

- "Two others, who were criminals, were led away to be put to death with him. And when they came to the place that is called The Skull, there they crucified him, and the criminals, one on his right and one on his left. And Jesus said, 'Father, forgive them, for they know not what they do.' (Lk. 23:32–34b)

TAKE ⑩

Choose one of the prayers of Jesus above and use it to inspire or inform a time of prayer today. Let one of his prayers lead you inward, outward, and upward in complaint, confidence, or compassion. And, remember, your prayer need not be perfect. Just say what you think and feel. God knows anyway, and he loves you always.

10

Using Paul's
Pre-Owned Prayers

A friend of mine lost his daughter a year and a half ago. A bubbly, joyful, and passionate woman of God, she died in a car accident hours after leaving my friend's arms for her college campus. And when she perished, so did my friend's prayer life. Mostly, he hasn't wanted to pray. But when he does want to, he can't seem to find the words. At my suggestion, he's started praying through some psalms. I'm hoping he'll find in these ancient prayers the words he can't find on his own.

This, in fact, is one of the benefits of praying Scripture. Richard Foster writes about the value of leaning on Scripture for supplication.[22] First, praying Scripture reminds us that we are part of a much larger community. As we pray words used by the body of Christ for centuries, we are reconnected with the global family of God. Second, the practice keeps us from giving in to the temptation to be spectacular and entertaining. By using words others have written, we don't have to worry about being clever, brilliant, or original. Third, praying Scripture breathes new life into our prayers as it stretches us with words and concepts with which we may be unfamiliar. But, perhaps most fundamentally, this habit provides words for issues and emotions we have no words for. Sometimes, we just don't know how to say what we want to say. Scripture often brings the very words we need. When we can't find our own words, these ageless words of others become a lifeline.

Eva Hermann spent two years in a Nazi prison camp. While there she learned prayer from a young cellmate. One of the practices that transformed her experience was praying Scripture. She wrote, "During many a walk in the courtyard I have permitted myself to be carried along by such a stream, by repeating again and again the words of a Psalm: for example Psalm No. 90, 'O God, Thou art our refuge and our strength.'"[23] She confessed that she met God in that prison camp in a way she had not met him anywhere else—not because of new and fresh words she discovered for prayer, but because of tried and tested words from Scripture.

Adele Calhoun observes, "Alongside the popularity of conversational prayer, with its up-to-the-minute spontaneity, stands the desire to be rooted in something ancient that has survived the centuries."[24] Praying Scripture roots us in this ancient world and tradition.

Praying Paul's Prayers

Many of Paul's letters include rich and rewarding prayers Paul uttered for his readers. By praying these prayers daily or weekly, we learn a new language and direction for prayer:

- "And it is my prayer that your love may abound more and more, with knowledge and all discernment, so that you may approve what is excellent, and so be pure and blameless for the day of Christ, filled with the fruit of righteousness that comes through Jesus Christ, to the glory and praise of God." (Phil. 1:9–11)

- "I do not cease to give thanks for you, remembering you in my prayers, that the God of our Lord Jesus Christ, the Father of glory, may give you the spirit of wisdom and of revelation in the knowledge of him, having the eyes of your hearts enlightened, that you may know what is the hope to which he has called you, what are the riches of his glorious inheritance in the saints, and what is the immeasurable greatness of his power toward us who believe, according to the working of his great might that he worked in Christ when he raised him from the dead and seated him at his right hand in the heavenly places, far above all rule and authority and power and dominion, and above every name that is named, not only in this age but also in the one to come." (Eph. 1:16–21)

- "For this reason I bow my knees before the Father, from whom every family in heaven and on earth is named, that according to the riches of his glory he may grant you to be strengthened with power through his Spirit in your inner being, so that Christ may dwell in your hearts through faith that you, being rooted and grounded in love, may have strength to comprehend with all the saints what is the breadth and length and height and depth, and to know the love of Christ that surpasses knowledge, that you may be filled with all the fullness of God." (Eph. 3:14–19)

• "And so, from the day we heard, we have not ceased to pray for you, asking that you may be filled with the knowledge of his will in all spiritual wisdom and understanding, so as to walk in a manner worthy of the Lord, fully pleasing to him, bearing fruit in every good work and increasing in the knowledge of God. May you be strengthened with all power, according to his glorious might, for all endurance and patience with joy, giving thanks to the Father, who has qualified you to share in the inheritance of the saints in light." (Col. 1:9–12)

Praying Paul's Lists

In each of the texts below, Paul provides a look at traits we should seek to eliminate from our lives and traits we should strive to emulate. Praying through these lists regularly helps us catch God's vision for our lives.

In Romans 12:9–21...

God, help me eliminate these traits: tolerating evil, being slothful, being haughty, being wise in my own sight, repaying evil with evil, being vengeful, being overcome by evil	God, help me emulate these traits: loving in a genuine way, holding on to the good, showing brotherly affection, showing honor, being fervent in spirit, being joyful, being patient, being prayerful, being generous, showing hospitality, blessing those who persecute me, living in harmony with others, associating with the lowly, doing what is honorable, living peaceably with others, overcoming evil with good

In 1 Corinthians 13:4–8...

God, help me eliminate these traits: being envious, being boastful, being arrogant, being rude, insisting on my own way, being irritable, being resentful, rejoicing at wrongdoing	God, help me emulate these traits: being patient, being kind, rejoicing with the truth, bearing all things, believing all things, hoping all things, enduring all things, never quitting

In Galatians 5:16–23...

God, help me eliminate these traits: being sexually immoral, being impure, being lustful, practicing idolatry, getting involved in sorcery, being full of enmity, promoting strife, being jealous, engaging in fits of anger, promoting rivalries, being involved in dissensions, causing divisions, being envious, getting drunk, being involved in orgies	God, help me emulate these traits: being loving, having joy, being peaceful, showing patience, being kind, being good, being faithful, being gentle, being self-controlled

In Colossians 3:5–14...

God, help me eliminate these traits: being sexually immoral, being impure, being controlled by passions, having evil desires, coveting, being angry, being wrathful, acting maliciously, being involved in slander, speaking obscenities, lying	God, help me emulate these traits: being compassionate, showing kindness, being humble, being meek, demonstrating patience, bearing with others, forgiving others, loving

TAKE ⑩

Choose one list or prayer from Paul and spend ten minutes using these words to speak to God. If you pray through a prayer list, pause at each quality or trait. Imagine God ridding you of that specific negative characteristic. Envision what your life would be like today if God granted you that positive trait. If you spend time in one of Paul's prayers, make the prayer your own. Turn his language of "you" and "yours" to "me" and "mine." Try to use as much of Paul's language as possible. But transform the prayer so that it truly speaks for you.

11

Hearing Heaven's Voice

Our fourth-grader recently inquired, "Why did you and Mom discipline me so much when I was younger?" Don't worry. We weren't abusive parents. And Jacob wasn't a troublesome child. It's just that, in comparison to his older sister, Jacob required a little more "motivation" early on in order to get him to stop bad behaviors and start desired deeds. We could unintentionally break his sister's heart with a firm "No!" But it took an earthquake to even get Jacob's attention.

One of Jacob's chief challenges was *listening*. Without any doubt, his ears performed perfectly. When we asked him to do something (e.g., "Jacob, please make your bed"; "Jacob, please quit bouncing that ball in the house"), the sound waves of our words played their intended tune on his eardrums, and they bounced their way into his brain. In spite of this, his bed remained unmade and that ball kept bouncing.

Jacob heard us. But he didn't really *hear* us.

This, it appears, is not a common struggle only for spirited elementary-aged boys. It is also one of the most common struggles for those of us desiring deeper spiritual lives. In her book *When the Soul Listens*, Jan Johnson surveys situations in Scripture when certain people were praised and others were condemned. The primary thing separating those commended from those critiqued was the ability or willingness to hear God.[25] For example, God scolded Israel in Isa. 42:20 "He sees many things, but does not observe them; his ears are open, but he does not hear." Jesus repeatedly invited "If anyone has ears, let him hear" (e.g., Mk. 4). The Bible is filled with appeals to hear God and admonitions against not hearing God. It's not that people are physically deaf, and are being invited to receive auditory healing. Their ears perform just fine. When God speaks or writes his words and people hear them with their ears or read them with their eyes, they wind up in their brains.

We hear God. However, sometimes we don't really *hear*–pay attention to and obey.

Jesus diagnoses his audience in his Sermon on the Mount as having this very problem. Repeatedly, Jesus says, "You have heard... but I say to you" (e.g., Mt. 5:21–22, 27–28, 31–32). In many of these cases, Jesus is referring to a specific scriptural passage that his listeners knew well. They had read this text. Studied it. Dissected it. Memorized it. Quoted it. But they hadn't really *heard* it. They understood the letter of the law, but they remained deaf to the spirit of the law. What Jesus attempts to do in his Sermon on the Mount is get us to hear God once more. Really hear.

Hearing God Through *Lectio Divina*

Thankfully, there is an ancient method that can empower us to hear Scripture as God desires. The early Christians discovered a way to listen closely to God. They believed Scripture was not merely a record of what God had once said. They trusted it was also the record of what God was now saying. To them the Bible was not a dusty diary of words God spoke to other people in past times. It was a living log of words God was speaking to them at the present time. And one specific approach enabled them to hear God through the text. The practice is called *lectio divina* (pronounced lex-ee-o dih-vee-nah). The phrase literally means holy or sacred reading.

While its roots run deep in both Old and New Testaments,[26] *lectio divina* was popularized by a man named Saint Benedict (ca. 480–550).[27] While attending school in Rome, Benedict became appalled at the sin running rampant throughout the ancient city. He determined to create an opportunity for people to experience a different life–an existence free from the epidemic of evil and filled with the countermeasure of consecration. Benedict retreated to a village, attracted bands of people dissatisfied with their spiritual status quo, organized them into monasteries, and created a guide for their living called *The Rule of St. Benedict* (published ca. 540). This guide spelled out the three primary activities through which people could enter into a life of sanctity and piety: prayer, work, and *lectio divina*. Benedict believed that one of the most fundamental ways to lead people into the deeper life of the Spirit was to guide them into a consistent practice of *lectio divina*. Why? Because it was one of the best ways of enabling people to hear God. Really hear God. And Benedict believed if people could truly listen to God, they would be forever changed.

What Benedict popularized, a man named Guigo II systematized (ca. 1115–1198).[28] In one of his books Guigo described the four rungs of a ladder by which people could be "lifted up from the earth into heaven." These four steps allowed an individual to listen deeply to God through *lectio divina*: (1) *lectio* (lex-ee-o),(2) *meditatio* (med-ita-tsee-o), (3) *oratio* (o-ra-tsee-o) and (4) *contemplatio* (con-tem-pla-tsee-o). Participation in each of these four activities would open up spiritual ears and enable us to hear what the living God is saying to us today. I've reworded these four steps below as (1) read, (2) reflect, (3) respond, and (4) rest.

TAKE ⑩

Take ten minutes today to experience this ancient practice. Through faith, trust that as you move through the four steps of *lectio divina*, you will hear God communicating to you in new and fresh ways.

Read

Lectio involves reading Scripture. First, select a biblical text. Choose one that is just a few verses in length. Before reading it, get into a comfortable position and maintain silence for several minutes. This prepares your heart to listen. Now, read the text slowly. Savor each word. To help you hear every sentence, consider reading each one out loud. When finished, read the passage two or three additional times. As you slowly read, be sensitive for one word or a phrase that sticks out and begs for more of your attention. Your goal is to hear one word or phrase that speaks to you or that piques your interest. Keep reading until this word or phrase comes to you.

Reflect

In *meditatio* you now reflect on this word or phrase. Slowly repeat the word or phrase that has caught your attention. Meditate on it. Chew on it. If you keep a journal, write the word or phrase there. Ask questions of it: "Why did this word or phrase catch my attention?"; "What is it about my life that needs to hear this word today?" Your goal is to identify why God has placed this word or phrase on your heart and what he may be asking you to do or be through it. Is he calling for some action? Is he requiring some repentance? Is he granting some insight? Is he highlighting a reason for praise?

Respond

In *oratio* you respond to what you've heard from God. By means of the word or phrase you've identified, God has spoken to you. Now, you speak to him. If God has convicted you of sin, respond with prayerful repentance. If he has given you a new understanding about something, respond with prayerful gratitude. If he has called you to action, respond with a verbal commitment to begin the action.

Rest

Finally, in *contemplatio,* you rest. Just as you began with a few moments of silence, so now finish this heavenly conversation the same way. Be quiet and still. Rest in the grace and presence of God.

12

Reading for Change

Longing to Listen

A former member of our congregation stopped by our church office recently. "What's going on?" I asked her. "Well," she said, "I finally retired. But now I'm not sure what to do. I guess I'm in a season of discernment. I'm trying to listen to God and discover what he wants me to do next."

In some ways, her description of her life stage fits many of us. For those who are truly seeking a more significant spiritual life, listening seems to be the one commonality. We're listening for God's guidance in our work. We're listening for his leadership in our relationships. We're listening for his direction in major decisions. We're listening for his answers to circumstances that puzzle us. For more and more of us, life with Jesus is a life of listening.

In his book *The Power of a Whisper,* pastor Bill Hybels focuses on about twenty individuals in the Bible who heard God in a distinct way.[29] These include Adam and Eve, Abraham, Jacob, Moses, Balaam, Joshua, Samuel, Job, Zechariah, Joseph, Mary, Jesus, Philip, Peter, and Paul. Each was blessed with direct interaction with and instruction from God. Each heard from the Lord. Many of us long for this very thing. We hunger for a fresh and living word from the One who made us and loves us.

The Power of the Heard Word

Thankfully, this craving can be satisfied through the meditative reading of Scripture. Marjorie Thompson calls this "spiritual reading":

Spiritual reading is reflective and prayerful. It is concerned not with speed or volume but with depth and receptivity. That is because the purpose of spiritual reading is to open ourselves to *how God may be speaking to us in and through any particular text.* The manner of spiritual reading is like drinking in the words of a love letter or pondering the meaning of a poem. It is not like skittering over the surface of a popular magazine or plowing through a computer manual. We are seeking not merely information but formation.[30]

The meditative reading of Scripture is one of the most promising ways to perceive the hushed voice of God. It is based on a singular conviction: God still speaks. He is not mute or silent. God has not lost his voice. We, on the other hand, too often have lost our ears. Just as he did to Adam, Moses, and Mary, so God still addresses any person who humbly seeks an audience with him in the pages of his word. He may express himself in many other ways. But most certainly he does so through the words of the Bible.

And this word, when heard, becomes a transformative power within us. Minister Mark Buchanan explains: "If this stuff gets in you, down in your guts, it is going to shape you in ways beyond your asking or imagination."[31] The more we heed God's voice in Scripture, the more it works its way inside us and reshapes us.

I've seen this stuff at work. My friends Nathan and Karen were teachers in local Memphis public schools. They were also voracious consumers of Scripture and intent on listening to God. One day they asked to meet with the staff and elders of our congregation. With great courage and conviction they announced, "We believe God has called us to move to the Philippines to become missionaries." Nathan's mother and father had been laboring for decades in the Philippines starting churches and establishing a highly respected school in the city of Bacolod. Nathan and Karen discerned that God wanted them to pack up their home, their two boys, and move thousands of miles to partner with the older Luthers in this work. As our church staff and elders prayed about this move and ministry, we reached the same conclusion. We sent Nathan and Karen to get additional training and then watched them fly away to a completely different life. I recently returned from visiting them and their work in the Philippines. Churches were thriving. Their school was overflowing. Life after life was changing. How did this all happen? I believe it started when that word got down inside Nathan and Karen and shaped them beyond their asking or imagination. Because they heard (and heeded), they– and the lives of many others–were forever changed.

Jesus affirms the power of the word in his Sermon on the Mount. As a concluding exhortation, he describes what happens to the person "who *hears* these words of mine and *does* them" (Mt. 7:24a). (Jesus believes real hearing always leads to heeding.) That person is changed into something akin to a house resting on a solid foundation that cannot be shaken despite the strongest storms (Mt. 7:24–25). Today you may feel like a shack likely to fall at the first sign of showers. You may see yourself as a hut about to collapse from a single clap of thunder. But if you learn to listen to Jesus, you will be transformed into a solidly constructed and firmly founded home that remains immovable and impenetrable even in the wildest weather.

Lectio divina is the ancient method of hearing the renovating, revolutionary, and foundation-building word of God. It is a method for gaining our lost ears so we may once again listen to the ever-speaking Father, Son, and Spirit.

TAKE ⑩

Set aside just ten minutes today to experience this powerful practice. Don't put it off. Do it right now if you can. Listen carefully. Let that word get down inside of you and change you in ways you never even dreamed of. Follow these simple, yet life-changing, steps.

First, choose a brief text of Scripture and *read* it. Read as if you are reading a letter from someone you deeply love. Read as if you are reading these words for the very first time. As you read, ask, "God, what do you wish to say to me today?" Listen for a word or phrase that seems to get stuck in your mind or impressed on your heart.

Second, begin to *reflect* on that word or phrase. Repeat it. Write it down. Draw something that represents it. Interrogate it: "What's going on in my life that would cause this word to stick out today? What sin am I wrestling with that this word addresses? What blind spot do I possess that this word illuminates? What comfort am I seeking or courage am I needing that this word brings? What is it about who I am right now that needs this word?"

Third, *respond* to God in prayer based on what you've heard. Give a shout of praise. Kneel in humble repentance. Thank him for the insight. Ask him further questions.

Finally, *rest* in the presence of God. Spend a few moments in quiet and calming silence with the Father who's shared so intimately with you today.

13

Direction from Above

Fresh out of college, Priscilla Shirer landed a job hosting a live televised show on CBS.[32] Shirer was a nervous wreck. She had little experience in live TV. And there were no opportunities for retakes. After all, it was *live*. Shirer was consumed with worry. *What if my train of thought derails on air? What if my mind goes blank in front of the camera?*

Sensing Shirer's trepidation, the producer handed her a small device that fit in her ear. The producer called the equipment "the ear." Though hidden from viewers, it would allow Shirer to hear the producer. No matter the circumstance, the producer could guide Shirer through it.

How I long for something like "the ear"! If only I could hear *the* Producer's voice no matter the circumstance. When I'm in pastoral counseling and don't know what to say to make a person's problem better. When I'm in a meeting about a critical issue and can't discern the best way forward. When I'm stuck in sermon preparation and have no idea where to go. When my kids ask a question I can't answer. When an unexpected job offer arrives and I don't know what to do with it. When I can't figure out how to exit the fast lane I'm stuck in. When a long-time member approaches me and I suddenly forget her name (which happens more than I care to admit). I think I could wear "the ear" out. Couldn't you? I'm certain most of us long for greater guidance from the One who is all-knowing and all-seeing.

I recently saw a cartoon in which a family with a young boy was exiting a church service. A sign on the wall told the title of the sermon that had just concluded: "God is omnipresent, omniscient, and omnipotent." Looking up at the preacher, the young boy said, "So, God is kind of like Google?" Yes, but to an infinite degree better.

What a blessing it would be to have a direct connection to this divine and caring source of guidance and direction!

Many Voices

Jesus frames himself as something like "the ear." Perhaps it's more appropriate to say he identifies himself as "the voice." In describing his desired relationship with us, Jesus is one who "calls" us "by name" (Jn. 10:3). We are those who "hear his voice" and "know his voice" (Jn. 10:3, 4, 16). The goal of discipleship according to Jesus is to hear and heed his voice and to disregard and discount every other voice (Jn. 10:4–5). Jesus states that there are two "ears." One carries the hushed and honest voice of Jesus. The second one carries the deafening and devious voices of others. Jesus' voice leads to abundant life (Jn. 10:10). The other voices lead to scarcity and fatality (Jn. 10:10).

How do we turn up the former and tune out the latter? This is the purpose of *lectio divina*. It provides a pathway for closing our ears to the glaring voices around us and opening our ears to the guiding voice of Father, Son, and Spirit. *Lectio divina* believes that the divine voice can still be heard "live" through Scripture. Richard Foster writes, "Whereas the *study* of Scripture centers on exegesis, the *meditation* of Scripture centers in internalizing and personalizing the passage. The written Word becomes a living word addressed to you."[33] By meditating on the word, we begin to hear the Voice. The ancient word spoken to generations in the past becomes a fresh word addressed to us in the present.

The One Voice

On most weekday mornings, I practice *lectio divina* on the text selected for my next sermon. A few weeks ago I was meditating on a passage in Luke 3. After *reading* it slowly and repeatedly, what caught my attention was that the word of God, absent for over 460 years, came to a man named John. God's word didn't come to the civic leaders mentioned in the narrative—men such as Tiberius Caesar or Pontius Pilate. It wasn't even delivered to the religious professionals highlighted in the story, such as Annas and Caiaphas. The word came to a relative nobody named John.

As I *reflected* on this, I started wondering why. Why did this word come to John and not to the others? Were the civic leaders too secular to receive sacred communication? Were the religious professionals too dead to hear this living word? Then I started wondering about myself—because I am a religious professional. I wondered what I could do to make sure I was more like John—someone who heard from God—and less like Annas and Caiaphas—men who got their paycheck from religion but didn't get a word from God. And I heard God challenging me that morning. This text came alive and grew into a fresh message from the Father. I heard something like this: "Chris, make sure you keep your heart and mind in a place where my word can find you. Don't assume that just because you are a religious professional, you'll hear my word."

I *responded* for a few seconds in prayer—confessing and repenting of those things that keep my ears dull and prevent me from hearing God's constant communication. Then I *rested* briefly in God's presence—humble yet grateful for the exchange we had just shared.

TAKE ⑩

God has something to say to you today. Take ten minutes and practice *lectio divina* on a brief biblical text. Invite God to speak clearly to you through those words. You may be surprised at just how clear his message becomes.

14

Putting an End to Words

Active Prayer

My family and I attend a small group that at one time focused on the prayer life of Jesus. After a convicting conversation, several of us confessed a desire to spend more time in prayer–to prioritize prayer like Jesus. Then one group member wondered aloud: "I want to pray more. But honestly, I don't know how I'd fill the time. I'm not sure what else I could say. I usually get through my prayer list in a matter of minutes. I'd quickly run out of things to pray." Like many of us, she wished for longer periods of prayer. But, like many of us, she questioned how she'd use the time if she actually had it.

This dilemma is the result of a particular view of prayer. One perspective sees prayer primarily as *active asking*. Prayer, for many, is an active, not passive, experience. We are physically active: our hands fold, our head bows, our knees bend, our mouth opens, and our tongue moves. We are also mentally active: we scan over and make supplication regarding a list of needs, requests, issues, and topics. We find it difficult to envision any model of prayer besides that in which we are the active participant and God is the passive recipient. Thus, when it comes to increasing the amount of time in prayer, we can only imagine increasing the amount of activity in prayer. We'll need to find more things to request, more people to intercede for, more topics of conversation to process, and more issues requiring God's divine intervention.

There are some positive points to this paradigm. For example, a swift scan of the prayers in Psalms and the prayers of Jesus and Paul reveals a plethora of pleas that they regularly made but which we rarely pray. It would be a life-shaping (and world-changing) experience to fill greater time praying over the things that concerned these masters of prayer. Hours could be added to our times with God if we simply started praying over lists like the ones found in Scripture.

Yet prayer has another side. God did not envision prayer solely as us actively asking and him passively receiving. God imagined the flipside of this paradigm as well. There is a way to approach prayer in which God is active and we are passive.

Wordless Prayer

The book of Psalms unleashes a literal revolution when it comes to prayer. It turns our idea about prayer on its head. Rather than prayer consisting of us actively asking and God passively receiving our requests, the psalter also imagines prayer as us resting passively while God takes the active role. Instead of prayer being chatty, Psalms envisions prayer being silent. Specifically, in contrast to the asking and talking that characterizes so much of our prayer lives, the psalter presents prayer as wordless:

- Psalm 4:4 – "Be angry, and do not sin; / ponder in your own hearts on your beds, and be *silent.*"
- Psalm 23:2 – "He makes me lie down in green pastures. / He leads me beside *still* waters."
- Psalm 37:7 – "Be *still* before the LORD and wait patiently for him; / fret not yourself over the one who prospers in his way, / over the man who carries out evil devices!"
- Psalm 46:10 – "Be *still,* and know that I am God. / I will be exalted among the nations, / I will be exalted in the earth!"
- Psalm 62:1, 5 – "For God alone my soul waits in *silence*; / from him comes my salvation... / For God alone, O my soul, wait in *silence,* / for my hope is from him."
- Psalm 131:1–2 – "O LORD, my heart is not lifted up; / my eyes are not raised too high; / I do not occupy myself with things / too great and too marvelous for me. / But I have calmed and *quieted* my soul, / like a weaned child with its mother; / like a weaned child is my soul within me." *(Emphasis was added in all quotes above.)*

Notice the impact of this wordless prayer. It conquers sinful anger (Ps. 4:4). It brings peace and contentment (Ps. 23:2). It frees us from having to be in control (Ps. 37:7). It creates an environment in which we experience the presence and sovereignty of God (Ps. 46:10). It enables us to see and sense God's salvation (Ps. 62:1, 5). It empowers us to find fulfillment completely in God (Ps. 131:1–2).

What might it be like to begin practicing a type of prayer that uses no words at all?

Waiting Prayer

But there's even more to this upside-down prayer paradigm. Not only does the book of Psalms contrast our chatty prayers with wordless prayers. It also contrasts our often obsessive activity in prayer with a surprising passivity. In the psalter prayer is not only wordless in nature, but waiting in nature:

- Psalm 25:3 – "Indeed, none who *wait* for you shall be put to shame; / they shall be ashamed who are wantonly treacherous."
- Psalm 25:5 – "Lead me in your truth and teach me, / for you are the God of my salvation; / for you I *wait* all the day long."
- Psalm 25:21 – "May integrity and uprightness preserve me, / for I *wait* for you."
- Psalm 27:14 – " *Wait* for the LORD; / be strong, and let your heart take courage; / *wait* for the LORD!"
- Psalm 31:24 – "Be strong, and let your heart take courage, / all you who *wait* for the LORD!"
- Psalm 33:20 – "Our soul *waits* for the LORD; / he is our help and our shield."
- Psalm 37:7 – "Be *still* before the LORD and *wait* patiently for him; / fret not yourself over the one who prospers in his way, / over the man who carries out evil devices!"
- Psalm 37:9 – "For the evildoers shall be cut off, / but those who *wait* for the LORD shall inherit the land."
- Psalm 37:34 – " *Wait* for the LORD and keep his way, / and he will exalt you to inherit the land; / you will look on when the wicked are cut off."
- Psalm 38:15 – "But for you, O LORD, do I *wait*; / it is you, O Lord my God, who will answer."
- Psalm 39:7 – "And now, O LORD, for what do I *wait*? / My hope is in you."
- Psalm 40:1 – "I *waited* patiently for the LORD; / he inclined to me and heard my cry."
- Psalm 52:9 – "I will thank you forever, / because you have done it. / I will *wait* for your name, for it is good, / in the presence of the godly."
- Psalm 62:1, 5 – "For God alone my soul *waits* in *silence*; / from him comes my salvation / For God alone, O my soul, *wait* in *silence*, / for my hope is from him."

- Psalm 130:5 – "I *wait* for the LORD, my soul *waits*, / and in his word I hope."
- Psalm 130:6 – "My soul *waits* for the Lord / more than watchmen for the morning, / more than watchmen for the morning." *(Emphasis was added in all quotes above.)*

Waiting is counterintuitive. Many of us still operate on a don't-just-stand-there-do-something mentality. Waiting is too dependent for us independent people. Yet notice the fruits of waiting. Courage comes as we wait (Ps. 27:14). God answers as we wait (Ps. 38:15). Hope arrives as we wait (Ps. 39:7). Prayer for these ancient masters was not only wordless but waiting.

In fact, twice a psalmist ties waiting and wordless together:

- Psalm 37:7a – "Be *still* before the LORD and *wait* patiently for him."
- Psalm 62:1, 5 – "For God alone my soul *waits* in *silence*; / from him comes my salvation / For God alone, O my soul, *wait* in *silence*, / for my hope is from him." *(Emphasis was added in quotes above.)*

What might prayer be like if you did more waiting and less acting?

Prayer as Restful Receiving

The description of prayer in Psalms offers a new paradigm. Rather than prayer being solely "active asking," prayer can also be "restful receiving." Here, prayer is not acting; it is resting. Here, prayer is not asking; it is receiving. There is a mode of prayer in which prayer is less about what we are doing and more about what is being done to us. We rest in the Lord. We are quiet and still in his presence. We calmly wait—for knowledge of him, for action from him, for a word from him.

This type of prayer has become known as contemplative prayer. In a nutshell, contemplative prayer is spending intentional time in silence with God. In a phrase, it is restful receiving. It can be for the sole purpose of *resting* in God and just being with God.

But silence can be for the additional purpose of *receiving* something from God—knowledge of God, a word from God, some action of God's. As a Father, God loves to just "hang out" with us—no agendas needed and no topics demanding conversation. And as a Father, God loves to give to his children. He has insight to provide, guidance to grant, and transformation to give. All of this, and more, can be gained through times of stillness and silence.

TAKE ⑩

Take ten minutes today—at home, on a walk, during a work break—and just spend ten minutes in silence. Begin by briefly telling God that you want to just rest in him and you want to receive anything he wishes to give in this time. Then, just sit. Be still. And wait on the Lord.

15

Saving the Most Endangered Species

Jesus hints at out need for silence in his Sermon on the Mount. Over and over Jesus chides us for hearing superficially rather than deeply. He says, "You have heard that it was said... But I say to you." Jesus says this six times. He's claiming that we are people who have heard about God and heard from Scripture, but we've not really heard deeply. And Jesus has come to challenge us to be better listeners. He warns us that we have a hearing problem. And the only way to truly hear better is to be quieter. In fact, to be silent.

The Bible records how followers of God turned to silence in times of trouble. Wrestling with suffering, David writes, "For God alone my soul waits in silence" (Ps. 62:1a). The author of Psalm 46 writes of trouble and then quotes God: "Be still, and know that I am God" (Ps. 46:10a). And in the midst of distress and doubt, David advises, "Ponder in your own hearts on your beds, and be silent" (Ps. 4:4b).

In Psalm 63, David recounts a time of intense trouble. His son Absalom plans a coup against David, and David is forced to flee from Jerusalem into the wilderness. He is stripped of his palace, his city, and his people. Cast into the stillness of the wilderness, he finds something—or rather someone. David finds God. In the quiet solitude of the wilderness, he is able to meditate on God. And though he has lost nearly everything, David writes that it's as if he is eating and drinking at a banquet there in the wilderness. What's he being filled with? God.

O God, you are my God; earnestly I seek you; / my soul thirsts for you; / my flesh faints for you, / as in a dry and weary land where there is no water. / So I have looked upon you in the sanctuary, / beholding your power and glory. / Because your steadfast love is better than life, / my lips will praise you. / So I will bless you as long as I live; / in your name I will lift up my hands.

My soul will be satisfied as with fat and rich food, / and my mouth will praise you with joyful lips, / when I remember you upon my bed, / and meditate on you in the watches of the night. (Ps. 63:1–6)

It's only when David is quiet in the wilderness that he realizes he is starving. And what he most needs is neither his palace nor his throne returned. What he most needs is God. And as he meditates upon God on his desert bed, as he meditates throughout the cold desert night about God, his soul is satisfied as if eating fat and rich food. Silence allows David to find true fulfillment in the midst of trials.

But the Bible records not only how God's people turned to silence in times of trouble. Silence was part of normal life for those in Scripture. In his most famous song, David writes of how God led him beside "still waters" (Ps. 23:2). One of the songs sung by the Israelites each time they travelled to Jerusalem urged them to calm and quiet their souls (Ps. 131:2). In one oft-quoted piece on the varieties of life, the author of Ecclesiastes writes, "For everything there is a season, and a time for every matter under heaven:...a time to keep silence, and a time to speak..." (Eccl. 3:1, 7b). The prophet Habakkuk urged, "But the LORD is in his holy temple; / let all the earth keep silence before him" (Hab. 2:20). For those whose lives and words are recorded in Scripture, silence was essential.

From Essential to Endangered

Today, however, silence has been overwhelmed by unrelenting noise. In 1920 a Nebraska inventor designed the first automobile alarm. In 2004 New Yorkers proposed a bill to ban car alarms as a public nuisance.[34] The two events are a telling commentary on our relationship with noise. At first we invite a little extra noise into our lives because it seems to serve a purposeful function. But then, like a cub grown into a lion, it takes over and resists all attempts to drive it out.

Noise, in fact, now comes standard with contemporary life. Gordon Hempton and John Grossmann introduce their book *One Square Inch of Silence* with these comments: " 'The day will come when man will have to fight noise as inexorably as cholera and the plague.' So said the Nobel Prize-winning bacteriologist Robert Koch in 1905. A century later, that day has drawn much nearer. Today silence has become an endangered species."[35]

Silence is truly an endangered species. One evening while I was leading a group discussion about silence and challenging those attending to spend ten minutes in silence the following day, one woman joked, "So, you can guarantee I'll actually get ten minutes of silence in my house?" She has three boys and holds two jobs. Silence is rare, measured more by moments than minutes. In fact, Richard Foster argues, "Distraction is the primary spiritual problem in our day."[36]

Perhaps it is for you as well. Yet silence must be invited, coaxed, and lured back into our lives. George Prochnick, author of *In Pursuit of Silence,* writes this in a *New York Times* op-ed:

> The scale of our noise problem isn't in doubt. In recent years rigorous studies on the health consequences of noise have indicated that noise elevates heart rate, blood pressure, vasoconstriction and stress hormone levels, and increases risk for heart attacks. These reports prove that even when we've become mentally habituated to noise, the damage it does to our physiologies continues unchecked... Rather than rant about noise, we need to create a passionate case for silence. Evidence for the benefits of silence continues to mount. Studies have demonstrated that silent meditation improves practitioners' ability to concentrate. Teachers able to introduce silence into classrooms report that it fosters learning and reflection among over-stimulated students. Professionals involved with conflict resolution have found that by incorporating times of silence into negotiations they've been able to foster empathy that inspires a peaceable end to disputes. The old idea of quiet zones around hospitals has found new validation in studies linking silence and healing... Unfortunately, in a world of diminishing natural retreats and amplifying electronic escapes, this delight is in ever shorter supply. The days when Thoreau could write of silence as "a universal refuge" and "inviolable asylum" are gone. With all our gadgetry punching up the volume at home, in entertainment zones and even places of worship, young people today often lack any haven for quiet.[37]

Behold, my beloved, I have shown you the power of silence, how thoroughly it heals and how fully pleasing it is to God. Wherefore I have written to you to show yourselves strong in this work you have undertaken, so that you may know it is by silence that the saints grew, that it was because of silence that the power of God dwelt in them, because of silence that the mysteries of God were known to them.46

Silence is gone. There are too few havens for quiet. Yet for those who seek the life Jesus came to bring, silence is essential. Although noise is now the default position for society, silence must be the default position for saints.

What Silence Is and Is Not

The discipline of silence or contemplative prayer is one step toward evicting the noise and embracing its opposite. But what is contemplative prayer? I've found that many Christians have fears or flawed understandings about it. Let's start the process of clarification by presenting three things silence is not.

First, silence is not a relaxation exercise.[38] The primary purpose of incorporating regular silence into our walk with God is not to depress blood pressure or decrease work, home, or school pressures. Without a doubt, your mind and body will feel more relaxed as a result of this discipline. But these are side benefits, not principal reasons for practicing silence. Our spiritual health, not merely our physical or emotional health, drives us to silence.

Second, silence is not a supernatural event in which God appears visibly or speaks audibly.[39] God *could* manifest himself in this way. But this is not the norm. Of the millions who have practiced silence, experiences like these are the exception. A few in the pages of the Bible or the annals of history were granted such encounters. Most were not. Carl McColman writes that before he embraced a life of practicing silence, he did normal things like washing the dishes and folding the laundry.[40] And after he began practicing silence? He says he continued to do normal things like washing the dishes and folding the laundry. What silence did was change how he experienced God in the midst of those normal things.

Third, silence is not an attempt to empty the mind. Emptying the mind is the purpose of Eastern meditation. But filling the mind is the purpose of Christian meditation.[41] We empty our setting of noise so we might fill our spirit with Christ.

What, then, is silence? It is a means of *resting* in God and *receiving* from him. The primary gift received is the presence of God. The silence clears away all distractions so that we can be fully present to the One who is always present. But, at times, we may also receive a word from God or some guidance from him. Ruth Haley Barton describes her life at one time as a jar of river water.[42] The busyness of life had stirred up all that sediment, making everything murky and cloudy. It was only when she began to practice silence that the sediment settled, the water cleared, and she was able to see the things God wanted to show her.

The Greek Church Fathers used the word *theoria* to describe an experiential knowledge of God. There's head knowledge of God. Then there's heart knowledge. There's knowing about God. And there's *knowing* God. This is *theoria*. The word *theoria* was eventually translated into Latin. This Latin word gave us the English word *contemplation*.[43] Thus, contemplative prayer, or silence, is a way to gain experiential knowledge of God. Silence transforms our head knowledge about God to heart knowledge of God. It's the difference between a wife reading a letter from her husband and the wife resting quietly and contentedly in her husband's arms.

A couple of additional images may help. First, imagine a car with an engine and a radio. We often hear the radio, but we rarely perceive the engine. In fact, the only time we notice the sound of the engine is when something goes wrong. The radio signifies all the urgent things that tend to capture our attention. The engine signifies God, who frequently goes unnoticed. Silence turns down the noise of the world (the radio) so we may attend to the voice and presence of God (the engine).[44]

Second, imagine a river flowing with water. On top of the water are boats and debris (tree branches, litter, etc.). We tend to focus on the floating objects while ignoring the ebb and flow of the water holding them up. The boats and debris signify all that distracts us, while the water stands for the God who sustains us, who keeps us afloat. Silence moves the eyes of our soul off the floating objects to the water underneath.[45]

Why Doing Nothing Is Doing Something

But does silence actually accomplish anything? More than we can imagine. For example, Peter of Celles wrote this in the Middle Ages: "God works in us while we rest in him. Beyond all grasping is this work of the Creator, itself creative, this rest. For such work exceeds all rest, in its tranquility. This rest, in its effect, shines forth as more productive than any work."[46] As we rest in him, God works in us. It is a retreat that ultimately proves to be more productive than any work we might do. The fruit of resting quietly in God will be borne throughout the rest of the day, the week, the month, and the year.

A fourth-century Desert Father wrote these words:

> Behold, my beloved, I have shown you the power of silence,
> how thoroughly it heals and how fully pleasing it is to God.
> Wherefore I have written to you to show yourselves strong
> in this work you have undertaken, so that you may know it is
> by silence that the saints grew, that it was because of silence
> that the power of God dwelt in them, because of silence that
> the mysteries of God were known to them.[47]

Silence "thoroughly heals." Silence is the means by which "the saints grew." Silence became the way in which "the power of God dwelt in them" and "the mysteries of God were known to them." Doing nothing may very well be the only way to truly do something.

Three Ways to Practice Silence

How do we incorporate silence as a spiritual practice? There are many ways, but here are three.

First, you can practice what I call "*simple silence.*" This involves incorporating silence into activities you are already doing. For example, my drive to work takes about twenty minutes each morning. During ten minutes of the drive, I listen to an audio version of the One Year Bible. For the remaining ten minutes, I drive in silence. It is intentional silence. I remind myself that God is present, and it is my desire to just spend that time resting in him. (Of course, I don't close my eyes!) I find that I am peaceful, sharp, and God-oriented once I arrive at the church building because of those few moments of silence.

Perhaps you walk, bike, or run for exercise. Consider spending at least part of that time in silence. No humming. No iPod. Just quiet. But be intentional. Remind yourself that God is with you and you desire to spend this time with him.

Or the next time it's your turn to wash the dishes, or make dinner, or do some other chore or household task, do it in silence. Remind yourself that God is present and you want to be present to him.

Second, you can engage in what I call "*single-minded silence.*" Here, you practice a period of silence because there is an issue on your mind you cannot ignore. Your mind seems fixated on it and you can't seem to ignore it. Thus, you enter a time of silence and symbolically set this issue before God. In silence you wait either for an answer or for assurance from God about the issue. You may receive guidance regarding the matter or you may receive a guarantee that God will be with you in the midst of the matter.

If you find yourself worried or anxious about something, take a few moments to verbalize that to God, and then sit in silence. God may communicate something to you. Or he may comfort you. If you find yourself needing to make a decision, verbalize that to God, then sit in silence. Be receptive to what God might communicate in that stillness.

Third, you can practice what I call "*serious silence.*" This is the formal version of contemplative prayer. Ideally, it consists of twenty minutes of silence at the beginning of the day and twenty minutes at the end of the day. The goal is not to hear from God, but to be with God and be present to him for a full twenty minutes. It takes at least this long for the average person's mind to stop grabbing onto random or demanding thoughts, memories, and feelings and to arrive at a state of true interior silence.

Sit with your eyes closed. No inspirational music. No humming. Just silence. In the silence your mind begins to wander. Rather than try to ignore those distracting thoughts, intentionally let go of them, as if releasing a stick and allowing it to float down the river. As each emotion or random thought comes, attend to it and let it drift down stream. The goal is to let these go and to just rest in the presence of God.[48] We are not trying to solve problems, process feelings, or understand issues. We are trying to intentionally spend twenty minutes in stillness with God.

TAKE ⑩

Take ten minutes today to practice *single-minded silence* or *serious silence.* If you are especially busy today, then just engage in some *simple silence* by incorporating true quiet time in an activity you are already doing.

16

Finding Power in a Pause

David had moments in life when he came to a place of weakness. A point of panic. A time of terror. An area of anxiety. Have you been there? Goliath may be the most famous incarnation of one of those instances for David. But there were others. Many others.

In Psalm 62, David journals about one of those other moments. We have no tradition suggesting when David wrote this psalm or to what situation it was addressed. Those are details we may never know (in this life). What we do know, however, is that the psalm describes David's descent to a position of powerlessness:

> How long will all of you attack a man
>   to batter him,
> like a leaning wall, a tottering fence?
> They only plan to thrust him down from his high position.
> They take pleasure in falsehood.
> They bless with their mouths,
>   but inwardly they curse. (Ps. 62:3–4)

David is being attacked. Not just by a man, but by a mob. David refers to "all" who are assaulting him. He describes a crowd battering him. He pictures himself as a leaning wall and a tottering fence. He is so fragile that he is about to topple over. He is so frail that he is about to go down for the count. This attack occurs when David is in a "high position." Perhaps he is already king, but these enemies seek to remove him from power. They seek his downfall. In public they may bless him, while in private they curse him. They cannot wait until he is gone for good.

Some of you can identify with the specifics of David's trial. Perhaps even this week someone has been attacking you. Unfairly.

Undeservedly. Unremittingly. You lie wounded and bruised. You feel like a leaning wall or a tottering fence.

Others of you can identify with the general nature of David's hurts. No person has been attacking you, but you still feel like you're in a war. The attack comes from a terrible temptation. Or a certain situation. Or a denied dream. You feel like you're going down for the count.

A Place of Strength

But as is so often the case, David does not remain in this place of weakness. Psalm 62 is the testimony of how he moves from a place of weakness to one of strength. Twice in the psalm David sings of newfound strength:

- "He alone is my rock and my salvation, / my fortress; I shall not be greatly shaken." (Ps. 62:2)
- "He only is my rock and my salvation, / my fortress; I shall not be shaken. / On God rests my salvation and my glory; / my mighty rock, my refuge is God. / Trust in him at all times, O people; / pour out your heart before him; / God is a refuge for us." (Ps. 62:6–8)

If David was once sinking in the sand, he's now resting on the rock. If he was once defenseless in the desert, he's now fixed firm in a fortress. If he was once fearful on the firing line, he's now recovering in a refuge. God has become his rock, his fortress, his refuge.

David has moved from a place of weakness to a place of strength.

It is possible for you to make a similar move. You too can transition from a place of weakness, hurt, shame, or pain to a position of strength, healing, confidence, and safety. You do not have to remain a leaning wall or a tottering fence. You do not have to go down for the count. You too can find a rock, a fortress, a refuge.

But the question is, "How?" How did David experience such a radical move in his life? And how do we journey from a place of weakness to a place of strength?

A Quiet Pause

David answers that question twice in this psalm:

- "For God alone my soul waits in silence; / from him comes my salvation." (Ps. 62:1)
- "For God alone, O my soul, wait in silence, / for my hope is from him." (Ps. 62:5)

To move from weakness to strength David did not do something. Instead, he did nothing. Twice he recounts how he waited in silence. Twice he boasts about ceasing all activity and simply resting. Twice he records stopping his feet, shutting his mouth, and just standing still.

Some scholars have thought that David is referencing a visit to a holy place. We don't know. What we do know is that it was only when David's movement stopped that his healing started. It was only when David's to-do list was lost that his spiritual vitality was found. It was only when David did nothing that God began to do everything.

The movement from weakness to strength comes in three simple words: Wait in silence. The more we learn to wait in silence, the more we gain strength, courage, and life. It can come in many forms: for example, spending a few minutes in quiet at the beginning or end of each day, reserving a half day each week for Sabbath with God, or planning a yearly retreat to a place of solitude and rest. But there is no escaping this fundamental fact: strength comes when we wait in silence.

Our Need for Silence

Tony Jones observes, "All in all, no spiritual discipline is more universally acclaimed as necessary than the practice of silence. The Desert Fathers retreated to the wild lands of Egypt; Rufinus, who toured the desert to visit as many of the Fathers as he could, wrote to Jerome, 'There is a huge silence and a great quiet here.'… Likewise, Benedict fashioned much of his Rule around the keeping of silence… Present day spiritual writers commend silence as well."[49] Silence is essential to our growth in piety.

Yet silence can be one of the hardest practices to embrace, as Gary Holloway explains: "For many of us, the hardest thing we can imagine doing is to do nothing. We have been taught from childhood to be busy, filling each moment of the day with activity. Our churches often teach us that to waste time is sinful. We should always be working for the Lord… Everyone knows that the more you work and the harder you try, the more you accomplish. Even in the spiritual life… Everyone knows that but God."[50] Similarly, Adele Calhoun comments, "When we come upon silence, we fill it. We cram it with something else we can learn or do or achieve. We break the silence of travel with an iPod, the silence of the evening hours with the TV or computer, the silence of sleep with an alarm clock. Every part of our life is inundated with words—urgent words, random words, trivial words, hurtful words, managing words, religious words, and on and on."[51]

In this world of noise, busyness, and addiction to words, we need quiet and wordless time with God. Primarily during this "nothing" time, we "are attending to him who loves us, who is near to us, and who draws us to himself."[52] The basic goal of silence is "to free myself from the addiction to and distraction of noise so I can be totally present to the Lord."[53] Only in this silence will we find the strength that David found.

Expectations

What can we expect from this time? Contemplative Thomas Keating urges us to come with few expectations and to come in the posture of a beginner:

> One cannot begin to face the real difficulties of the life of prayer and meditation unless one is first perfectly content to be a beginner and really experience himself as one who knows little or nothing, and has a desperate need to learn the bare rudiments. Those who think they "know" from the beginning will never, in fact, come to know anything... We do not want to be beginners. But let us be convinced of the fact that we will never be anything else but beginners, all our life![54]

We come to silence with few expectations, and in the humility of those who are constantly learning to practice and receive the benefits of silence.

Still, there are certain realities about silence that most of us will encounter when we begin to practice this discipline. Gary Holloway reveals three of these:[55]

- First, you might feel some physical or emotional pain. Difficult emotions and suppressed experiences may suddenly surface. (Indeed, as Adele Calhoun writes, silence can be a bit like a spiritual can opener: "Like a can opener the silence opens up the contents of your heart, allowing us deeper access to God than we experience at other times. As we remain in silence, the inner noise and chaos will begin to settle. Our capacity to open up wider and wider to God grows. The holy One has access to places we didn't even know exist in the midst of the hubbub."[56])
- Second, you might feel euphoria or deep joy as you are submerged in a peace beyond understanding and gain a sense of God's nearness.

- Third, you might feel nothing. You might begin to think silence is a waste of time. But silence is not about feeling. It is not about creating silence. Feelings may come. If so, embrace them as gifts or face them with God as challenges. You might feel nothing. That is also fine. Silence is not our attempt to be spiritual or create spiritual experiences. Instead, it is an act of pure faith. We trust that God blesses those who spend time with him. We believe, even when we do not see, that God is working in us in the silence.[57] Thomas Merton echoes this point: "If we bear with hardship in prayer and wait patiently for the time of grace, we may well discover that meditation and prayer are very joyful experiences. We should not, however, judge the value of our meditation by 'how we feel.'"[58]

Though, at times, we may wonder if our times in silence are "productive" or "useful," we must trust that God is at work in hidden and unknown ways during this time.

TAKE ⑩

Spend ten minutes in silence with God today. Here are some guidelines for the time:

1. Set a timer so you do not have to glance at a watch or a clock and thus interrupt the still time.
2. Begin by verbally telling God you want to draw near to him in this time of silence.
3. Sit upright, eyes closed, hands in your lap, feet on the floor (not crossed). You want to be comfortable enough that you are not distracted by a cramp or a limb falling asleep, but not so comfortable you fall asleep.
4. Within seconds your mind will feed you a myriad of thoughts and images. Choose a word, a sacred word, that you can silently express when each thought comes. This word is a way for you to let that thought go and center back upon God. Your word could be "Father" or "come" or anything you choose. The word should help you let that thought float down the river so that your attention remains on the river that is God.
5. Some people find it helpful to visualize something that symbolizes the presence of God. A friend of mine pictures sitting on a porch on a rocking chair and Jesus sitting next to him. You don't have to visualize. I rarely do. But if it's helpful, do so.

6. When the timer goes off, verbally thank God for this time with him. Some groups with whom I practice a time of silence close the time by repeating the Lord's Prayer aloud.

SECTION THREE

Gracious toward People

17

Placing Relationships
Back into Religion

During the 1992 U.S. presidential race, Democratic strategist James Carville walked into candidate's Bill Clinton's "War Room" and posted a note that read, "It's the economy, stupid!" The note was Carville's way of reminding the Clinton team of their top priority: the economy. A political campaign faces a number of seemingly important issues it may pursue. But Carville believed if Clinton kept the focus on how a vote for him was a vote for prosperity, Clinton would win the campaign. If your main thing is to make the main thing the main thing, you maximize your potential for success.

The same is true with life. Many of us face a number of seemingly important issues we may pursue with our time, talents, and treasures. For most of us, it's not that we can't decide what is good and what is bad. It's that we can't decide what is good and what is best. The Sermon on the Mount is Jesus' way of making the main thing the main thing. Jesus walks into our war room and posts a note: "It's piety! It's people! It's possessions!" Nothing else matters like loving God, loving neighbor, and blessing both with all we have. Make that our life's platform and we maximize our potential for genuine success.

The Move from Piety to People

There is a logical connection between piety, the focus of the previous section in this book, and people, the focus of this section. Piety, often envisioned as an inward-focused discipline, should naturally and ultimately flow into mercy and compassion toward others, frequently viewed as outward-focused disciplines. Tony Jones writes, "[F]or centuries, the Christians who were known for their service to the world were also those Christians who took their spiritual development seriously. When we take time and make space for God to move in our lives, we then have the resources necessary for true servanthood."[1]

The private disciplines of intimacy with God move naturally to public disciplines of service toward others. This is why I began this book with piety. We want to focus first on our walk with God and some of the related interior disciplines. These, however, are meant to turn us outward toward others. Closeness with God provides the resources for compassion for others. In this chapter we make this important turn.

When People Are First

What would it look like to put people first? What things would we do or not do if we decided to center our energies on others rather than ourselves? Jesus paints this life in the following lessons from his Sermon on the Mount:

- Show favor to the poor in spirit who have no one but God in their corner, the mournful so weary of the wrong in the world, the meek and those missing out, and those who are hungering and thirsting for the world to be made right. (Mt. 5:2–6)
- Show mercy. (5:7)
- Pursue God's peace for all people. (5:9)
- Do not harbor anger, but rather [would it be possible to weave in some synonyms for "rather"?] seek reconciliation. (5:21–26)
- Pay any price to think and act without lust. (5:27–30)
- Do not divorce, but rather be faithful. (5:31–32)
- Do not deceive, but rather let your "yes" mean "yes." (5:33–37)
- Do not respond to evil with violence, but rather with love. (5:38–48)
- Pursue the strengthening of your own weaknesses rather than pointing out the weaknesses of others. (7:1–6)
- Do to others what you would have them do to you. (7:12)
- Do not listen to others because of the fruit on their resumes, but rather because of the fruit in their character. (7:15–20)

Imagine the impact if, for just one week, you practiced this teaching in your home, office, classroom, neighborhood, or church. Imagine the influence if you took just one lesson from Jesus' list above and determined to apply it in every human interaction for one day. The experience would not only change the lives of the people around you. It would change yours as well.

The Discipline of Service

But how do we move in this direction? What Jesus calls for is challenging, daunting, even overwhelming. Look over that list again. Put a mental checkmark by the behaviors you regularly practice. Put a mental "x" by the ones you rarely practice. Are there more "x's" than checkmarks? There are for me. How do we increase the checkmarks? What first steps could we take to close the gap between the way we currently interact with others and the way Jesus dreams of us interacting with others? Service is one habit or discipline that can help.

Service as a spiritual discipline is different from service in general. Dallas Willard helps us see this: "I will often be able to serve another simply as an act of love and righteousness… But I may also serve another to train myself away from arrogance, possessiveness, envy, resentment, or covetousness. In that case, my service is undertaken as a discipline for the spiritual life."[2] We should always take advantage of spur-of-the-moment opportunities to serve as acts of love and righteousness. But the discipline of service involves planned and intentional deeds. We become deliberate and strategic about identifying acts of service that will train us away from things such as arrogance, possessiveness, envy, resentment, and covetousness. If we are particularly prideful, we seek an act of service that requires great humility. If we are unusually covetous, we strategize a deed that involves surrendering that for which we long. Each intentional act of service does two things: it inches us away from the sinfulness in our character, and it inches us toward the sinlessness of the Christ.

TAKE ⑩

Take ten minutes today to do two things. First, identify a sin in your life that is particularly vexing. Second, strategize an act of service that could attack that sin. If pride is a problem, plan an act of service in which you will receive no acclaim or credit. If greed is a vice, plan an act of service that will require you to give up something you value. Rise now and put that plan into action. In the next chapter, I'll give you an opportunity to turn your developed plan into a brick-and-mortar act of service.

18

Becoming a
Secret Service Agent

I once served as an apprentice at a Memphis congregation while I was a student at the Harding School of Theology. One summer the leaders of the congregation planned a road trip to a popular leadership seminar hosted by a large church. I wanted to attend but did not have the funds. My wife and I were literally pouring every cent we had into my studies. Days before the event, my supervisor Harold took me aside. "Someone's given me money so you can go with us!" he told me. All costs were covered. "Who is it?" I asked. "Who gave the money?" He wouldn't tell me. The donor wished to remain anonymous. I was overjoyed. The trip and seminar turned out to be refreshing and paradigm-shaping. I still feel the influence of that event as I minister today. And it was possible only because of an act of "secret service."

Mark Buchanan writes about the importance of secrecy in our acts of service:

> We want to be either heroes or martyrs. Our acts of service tend to rise from the yearning to be one or the other. We want to be either carried on the crowd's shoulders or trampled beneath the mob's feet...[E]mblazon my name on the marquee or set me ablaze at the stake... Make me a hero or make me a martyr... [But] God invites us, Christlike, to become servants. That means we'll do many of our acts of service in secret. We'll do them regardless of whether we're thanked or applauded. We'll do them not seeking persecution, but not avoiding it either.[3]

A problem for many us is that we want to do acts of service so striking that we are hailed as heroes, or acts of service so sacrificial that we are memorialized as martyrs. But some of the most impactful ways of serving are not so striking or sacrificial. One of the most transformative habits to cultivate is that of serving in ways that are commonplace and clandestine. Secret service doesn't necessarily make us heroes, because it isn't noteworthy enough to make the news. And it doesn't necessarily make us martyrs, because it isn't valuable enough to go viral. This is why secret service is so rare. Yet nothing imprints Christ upon our character like an act of anonymous aid to another.

The Shock of Secret Service

Secret service has transformative power because it runs so contrary to our fleshly desires. As Richard Foster tells us: "Of all the classical Spiritual Disciplines, service is the most conducive to the growth of humility... Nothing disciplines the inordinate desires of the flesh like service, and nothing transforms the desires of the flesh like serving in hiddenness. The flesh whines against service but screams against hidden service."[4] The more we practice hidden acts of kindness and sympathy, the more our flesh kicks and screams. It craves the attention and applause that can only come from public and advertised service. Most of us want to serve, as long as we get a mention on the ten o'clock news. But when service is hidden and secret, it forms us into people who look and love more like Jesus.

Secret service is, in the words of Dallas Willard, an act of trust: "Few things are more important in stabilizing our walk of faith than [secrecy]. In the practice of secrecy, we experience a continuing relationship with God independent of the opinions of others... Secrecy rightly practiced enables us to place our public relations department entirely in the hands of God..."[5] Many of us have our own PR department. We use it to broadcast an appealing image of ourselves to others. And some of the greatest branding tools our PR department has are our acts of service. Everyone loves a servant. Thus, we are tempted to plaster our compassionate conduct on billboards for all to see. Yet, when we serve secretly and anonymously, we spin off our PR department and place it in the hands of God. He alone takes over all branding decisions. We are free to focus solely on serving.

This, of course, is not easy to do. Theologian and spiritual formation author James Bryan Smith suggests that many of us live by the following narrative or story: "My value is determined by your assessment."[6] We hunger for affirmation and attention from others because it establishes our value. We believe there is no way to determine our worth other than the words people use to describe us. Thus we serve—but we serve in ways that bring attention to ourselves. What is needed, Smith writes, is a new narrative. He proposes this: "My value is determined by God's assessment." Because God's view of me is the only one that matters, I can now live for an audience of One. My worth is no longer dependent on what others think of me. Thus I am free now to serve, and to serve secretly.

TAKE ⑩

Take ten minutes to perform an act of secret service today. Serve in a way that allows you to remain anonymous. Tell no one about the act. Ask God to use this service, not only to bless the recipient, but to change you, the giver.

19

Getting Rid of Self-Service

Service in the Flesh

In a few months, my daughter will be taking a driver's education course to prepare her to become a licensed driver. Imagine if I picked her up, day after day, at the end of each day's instruction, and each time she shared a report like this: "We read again today about driving. We looked at several paintings about driving. We even closed our eyes and imagined driving."

"Did you get in a car and watch someone drive?" I might ask. "Did you actually get behind the wheel?"

"No," she might say. "The instructor doesn't really believe in doing things like that."

I'd demand a refund. You can't learn driving simply through instruction and imagination. You've got to see it fleshed out in front of you. And you've got to eventually get in the driver's seat yourself.

Perhaps this is why, in Matthew's Gospel, Jesus follows his greatest preaching with some of his greatest practice. In Matthew 5–7 Jesus gives verbal instruction about the journey of life. Then in chapters 8–10 he lives out what he has just talked about. Jesus cleanses a leper, heals the servant of a centurion, cures many, casts demons from two men, raises a paralytic, ends a woman's bleeding, restores life to a little girl, gives sight to two blind men, and enables a mute man to speak. For three chapters Jesus declares to us how to live. Then for three chapters he demonstrates for us what that life looks like. He not only teaches us about the priority of people; he shows us what it looks like to prioritize people. This is Jesus saying, "Here's a life lived for the sake of others. Go and do likewise."

Service in Many Forms

Jesus demonstrates service in the flesh. More specifically, he demonstrates service in its many forms. He practices service as cleansing, service as curing, and service as casting out. He practices service to a little girl, service to a lowly servant, and service to a leper. Service has a variety of shapes. Service is aimed at a variety of people. Jesus' life not only illustrates the persistent power of service but also the many modes of service.

John Ortberg spells out three general ways to practice service.[7] First, we can engage in "the ministry of the mundane"–simple acts of kindness that are more ordinary than extraordinary: comfort a crying child; assist someone stalled by the side of the road; pick up things that aren't ours and put them in their right place.

Second, we can engage in "the ministry of being interrupted"–being available for people who interrupt us when we don't feel available. While it can be spiritually healthy to make and keep schedules, we can also learn to be flexible and take care of someone's needs, even when that doesn't fit our timetable.

Third, we can practice "the ministry of holding your tongue." Rather than speaking up in a meeting to let everyone know how much we know, we can choose to be quiet. Rather than bragging to others about our accomplishments, we can refrain from talking.

Perhaps these are not what you think of when you think of serving. Yet they are as transformative as more stereotypical ways of serving. For example, last night my wife Kendra cooked one of her most famous meals: chicken fried steak, mashed potatoes, gravy, green beans, and rolls. All from scratch. Without any exaggeration I can say that it was a phenomenal meal. Unequalled. Not even American cook and TV celebrity Paula Dean could have matched it.

Preparing this masterpiece, however, makes a mess. And in our home we have a rule: if one spouse cooks, the other cleans. So after dinner, I dutifully began washing the line of dirty dishes that covered most of our kitchen counter. But rather than taking a well-deserved break, Kendra came by my side, grabbed a towel, and started drying. Together, we did the dishes in about half the time it would have taken me alone. This was a simple yet extremely significant act of service. It didn't require anything extraordinary, but it was very meaningful to me.

Adele Calhoun adds to Ortberg's list with additional ways to serve.[8] First, ask your spouse, roommate, or colleague every morning for two weeks, "What can I do for you today?" (One woman I know lives with a roommate. She recently started asking this question each morning, and it left her roommate speechless!) Second, develop a yearly practice of getting involved in one intentional service, mission, or relief project. Third, sign up to set up or take down after an event–the least sought after job at an event. Fourth, make a list of people whose services you receive (teachers, ministers, caretakers, etc.) and then do one thing for each of those people.

There are as many styles of service as there are personalities on the planet. Just pick one. And go serve.

Is It Authentic or Fake?

But before you pick, make sure you choose something that is true and genuine in nature. No matter the form, all true forms of service share certain characteristics. Richard Foster distinguishes true service from self-righteous service in the following ways:[9]

Self-Righteous Service	True Service
Self-righteous service is concerned with the "big deal" and only wants to engage in service that is titanic.	True service will act in both big and small ways.
Self-righteous service requires external rewards. It needs to know the service is appreciated and applauded.	True service is content with hidden and secret service. The service is its own reward.
Self-righteous service is highly concerned about results. If it cannot see fruit from the service, it quits the service.	True service shows compassion regardless of results.
Self-righteous service chooses who to serve. It engages only those who are deemed deserving.	True service is indiscriminate.
Self-righteous service depends upon moods. The person serves only when the mood strikes.	True service ministers regardless of mood.

No matter the type of service, true service is not concerned with the size of the act, is content to remain anonymous, does not worry about results, serves without partiality, and functions even when the giver does not feel like serving.

TAKE ⑩

Choose one type of service from the lists above and practice it today. No matter what specific form your service takes, make sure it remains an act of true service rather than self-righteous service.

20

Confessing Your Way
to Compassion

One day Rebecca Pippert attended two very different events: a graduate-level psychology class at Harvard University and a Christian Bible study nearby. Pippert observed a major difference in the way the two groups handled personal problems:

First, the students [in the graduate-level psychology class] were extraordinarily open and candid about their problems. It wasn't uncommon to hear them say, "I'm angry," "I'm afraid," "I'm jealous"... Second, their openness about their problems was matched only by their uncertainty about where to find resources to overcome them. Having confessed, for example, their inability to forgive someone who had hurt them, [they had no idea how to] resolve the problem by forgiving and being kind and generous instead of petty and vindictive. [But at the Bible study] no one spoke openly about his or her problems. There was a lot of talk about God's answers and promises, but very little about the participants and the problems they faced.[10]

Pippert reached this conclusion: "The first group [the psychology class] seemed to have all the problems and no answers; the second group [the Bible Study] had all the answers and no problems."[11]

Sadly, that is how some Christians perceive and deal with reality. They see the problems out there in the world and they have all the answers for them. But in here (the church) they see no problems and need no answers. Christians too readily recognize others' iniquity but too rarely recognize their own. We've got all the answers and none of the problems.

Confession and Compassion

The ability to confess our own corruption is critical to living the life Jesus imagined. Confession is especially essential if we wish to experience the kind of human connections Jesus envisioned. It's not just vital in religion. It's vital in relationships too.

Jesus paints a life in which we do not judge others but instead recognize our own flaws and limitations (Mt. 7:1–5). He further calls us to treat others in the way we wish to be treated (Mt. 7:12). Confession is a spiritual discipline that makes these qualities possible.

Many of us may automatically think of confession as a discipline designed to deepen our relationships with God. While true, it is also a habit calculated to change our relationships with people. Confession impacts relationships in two ways. Negatively, confession keeps us from judging the failures in the lives of others because it reminds us of our own failures. Positively, confession enables us to treat flawed people with the mercy with which we wish to be treated. The discipline of confession not only injects humility and honesty into our walk with God but meekness and mercy into our walk with people.

Confession does this by changing our story. James Bryan Smith writes that too many of us have bought into a false story that says, "I need to judge in order to fix someone or feel better about myself."[12] Smith clarifies what he means by "judging."[13] Judging is different than assessing. Judging is making a negative evaluation about a person without standing in solidarity with that individual, while assessing is simply evaluating a person's behavior. Judging makes a negative statement about the person, but assessing makes a negative statement about the behavior. Smith states that many of us judge others because we want to fix them or feel better about ourselves. We genuinely think that by pointing out another person's failures, we are actually helping them. Or we put people down in order to lift ourselves up. Either way, our narrative destroys our relationships. And Christians have an alarming tendency to do this. We Christians are too often known for the generosity of our judgments against others and the poverty of our passion for others.

One cure for this is confession. Confession changes our story. The more we confess to God and to others the flaws in ourselves, the less likely we are to criticize the flaws in others. Confession ultimately leads to compassion. Marjorie Thompson writes about this connection:

> The more clearly we see ourselves, the harder it becomes to judge the weaknesses and failures of others… As we perceive the realities of sin in ourselves, we can identify with the

brokenness of others. Instead of condemning someone whose behavior is irritating or unacceptable, we may recall similar behavior in our own lives. This doesn't make the behavior more palatable, but it gives us a different perspective on the wounds of the person behaving under compulsion.[14]

TAKE ⑩

Take ten minutes today to prayerfully evaluate your recent thoughts, motives, and actions. Identify some that are less than Christlike and acknowledge them to God. Receive his forgiveness. Allow it to flow over you and within you. Know that he loves you in spite of your struggles. Then leave, prepared to be more caring and sensitive regarding the flaws of others.

21

Seeing Yourself Through the Eyes of Others

When Howard Schultz resigned from Starbucks in 2000, the coffee chain was healthy and growing. Eight years later, the beverage behemoth was stumbling downhill. To halt the slide, Schultz stepped back in as CEO. In an interview about the return, Schultz said that before Starbucks could anticipate success, they had to admit their failures. Before they could experience transformation, they had to practice confession:

> When I returned in January 2008, things were actually worse than I'd thought. The decisions we made were very difficult, but first there had to be a time when we stood up in front of the entire company as leaders and made almost a confession— that the leadership had failed the 180,000 Starbucks people and their families. And even though I wasn't the CEO... I should have known better. I am responsible. We had to admit to ourselves and to the people of this company that we owned the mistakes that were made. Once we did, it was a powerful turning point. It's like when you have a secret and get it out: The burden is off your shoulders.[15]

It's only when we courageously confess that we've failed that a powerful turning point becomes possible. Our success in the future relies on our transparency about the past.

Characteristic Confession and Signature Sins

This is especially true when it comes to a certain class of sins. John Ortberg calls these "signature sins"—sins unique to each of us.[16]

Just as we have a one-of-a-kind pattern in our fingerprints, so we each have a unique pattern of sin. The temptations appealing to me may not be as appealing to you. What I struggle with most, you may struggle with least.

This signature sin, Ortberg argues, is tied to our signature strength. Our failures and fortes tend to have similar roots. For example, those with a gift of service tend to struggle most with the desire to be needed. Those who are strong leaders wrestle more often with the temptation to live for their image. Our greatest weakness is generally attached to our greatest strength.

This signature sin, I propose, may thus be the one most responsible for not only retarding our relationship with God but also ruining our relationships with others. If there is any sin in need of radical reconstructive surgery so that these relationships can be saved, it's this kind of sin.

What's called for, therefore, is "characteristic confession"– confession that is unique and characteristic only to you because it addresses a sin that is distinctive and descriptive only of you. Signature sins require characteristic confession. We must learn to pinpoint and then profess the sins that are so representative of our own unique failures and flaws.

Blind Spots

The great challenge with signature sins, however, is that they are difficult for us to see. Because they are so intertwined with our strengths and so imprinted on our hearts, they can be challenging for us to notice. What is sometimes painfully obvious to the other people in our life is often invisible to us.

Characteristic confession of signature sins thus sometimes necessitates the presence of another trusted and caring person. Others' seeing eyes can replace our blind eyes. We can ask them to look into our lives and reveal what they witness. They will likely be more able to identify our signature sins than we are.

But who do you pick for such a delicate and potentially frightening mission? After all, as Richard Foster points out, while theoretically any Christian can receive the confession of another, realistically not every Christian will have the empathy and understanding needed. Not every Christian will have the ability to keep your confidence. Not all will be wise enough to help you deal constructively with your signature sin. Thus, Foster urges, look for people with these qualities: (1) they evidence a deep faith in God's power to forgive; (2) they are filled with joy; (3) they are spiritually mature, wise, and compassionate;

(4) they have good common sense; and (5) they possess a good sense of humor.[17]

TAKE ⑩

If you already have a person like this in your life, spend ten minutes today with that person and ask: "What's my signature sin? What's my blind spot? What's the pattern of sin you most often see within me?" Receive the person's answer with humility and grace. Ask the person to pray for you at that moment, that God's Spirit might transform you. Leave that conversation with greater humility and compassion, ready to interact with others who wrestle with their own signature sins.

If you don't have a person like this in your life, take ten minutes today to make a list of people who might potentially serve in this capacity. Pray over the list and ask God for wisdom. Ask him to bring to you someone who might lovingly reveal to you your signature sin.

22

Eliminating Counterfeit Confession

Getting Real

What is confession? Mark Buchanan defines it this way: "Confession is presenting our real self to God. It's bringing before God not the person we hope to be, but the person we actually are… Confession is when we quit all the deal making, the sidestepping, the mask wearing, the pretense and preening, and we get bone-deep honest before God."[18] Confession is all about presenting our real self to God–and to the people around us. The more bone-deep honest we are with God and people about ourselves, the better. The less will be our pretense before God and preening in front of others, the greater will be our closeness to God and connection with people. Confession empowers us to be exactly who we are–in relationship with God and with others. And it is only by being who we are, not who we hope to be, that we can experience authentic attachments to God and others.

This type of honesty is challenging, yet it is what we ultimately long for. Christian psychologist Mark McMinn tells of one woman's failure to find honesty even in a loving home:

> She described her childhood in a home where self-esteem was the primary virtue. Her parents taught her that she was delightful, talented, good-hearted, intelligent, and witty. Having spent several months with her in a small group, I tended to agree with her parents… But as she talked about her spiritual awakening, she acknowledged that something important was missing from her incubator of childhood self-

esteem. Somehow, deep down, she always knew that she was not quite as great as her parents thought she was. She knew that there was an intrinsic need for healing, an inner darkness, a moral decay, which was also part of her character...What she longed for was authentic awareness of her good and bad qualities, and love that was big enough to embrace her regardless of her sin. When she turned to God as a young adult, she found what she had been longing for–One who knew every dark corner of her soul and still believed her to be worthy of love, forgiveness, and grace. Self-esteem and positive self-talk could not meet the deepest needs of her heart. A sound theology of sin and grace was her only hope.[19]

This woman ached for someone to concede what she already comprehended–that her perfection was terribly imperfect. She desired a faith or a figure that would point out her vice as well as her virtue. She dreamed of a God who comprehended the dark corners of her soul yet cared for her in spite of them.

Confession is the discipline that turns these desires into reality. Confession is not something God needs but what we need. The degree of transformation we experience from our sin is directly correlated with the degree of truthfulness we have about our sin. We hunger for honesty about ourselves because we hunger for healing for ourselves. Confession is the pathway to this healing. It's only when we acknowledge the cold darkness in our hearts that we can receive the warm light from God's heart.

Authentic Confession

Only true confession brings this type of transformation. When we explored the discipline of service earlier, we noted the distinction between authentic and inauthentic service. There is a similar distinction to be made as we consider confession. Marjorie Thompson proposes that genuine confession can be contrasted with counterfeit confession in two primary ways:[20]

	Genuine Confession	Counterfeit Confession
Focus	God	Failures
Result	Humility	Anxiety or Pride

The problem with counterfeit confession is that it leads to one of two destructive fruits: anxiety or pride. The more our attention is drawn only toward our failures, the more easily we fall into anxiety.

We begin to fret because we seem so unworthy of God's love. We start to despair because we see how flawed we truly are.

Counterfeit confession can also lead to pride. We may actually become conceited because of our confession. That is, we may grow proud at the way we've learned to be honest with God. ("Look at me, God. I admit my flaws frequently. I'm not like that Pharisee who could only admit the flaws of others!") We may also become proud of our sin. It can become a kind of badge of honor. ("No one struggles with this as much as I do. No one has such a burden of sin like mine!") Pride or anxiety is the result of counterfeit confession.

True confession, however, never bears these two deadly fruits. Its focus is on God rather than on us. It meditates much more on the Father than on our faults. It contemplates God's favor rather than just our fiascos. And, as a result, true confession bears the fruit of genuine humility that neither lifts us too high nor drops us too low. In true confession we receive an accurate portrait of who we are. But we also receive a correct image of who God is.

A college student named Jasmine modeled this for me one recent Sunday morning. She stepped hesitantly to the pulpit during our worship service. She had been asked to share her testimony prior to the congregation taking communion. Jasmine unfolded a sheet of paper and laid it on the pulpit. Her nervous hands, not knowing what to do, danced back and forth from her waist to the paper and back to her waist. "My freshman year was the lowest spiritual point of my life," she confessed. "My heart became so tarred with sin that nothing could scrub it clean." Jasmine explained the ways in which she had turned from God over that year. "But," she said, "I have learned that my vice is not greater than his sacrifice. No blemish is so deep it cannot be removed by his blood." Jasmine pointed us to the fruit of the vine and the unleavened bread of communion. She urged us to find cleansing and wholeness there, just as she had. Hers was one of those true confessions. By the time she finished, our thoughts centered not on the magnitude of her sin but on the mercy of her Savior.

TAKE ⑩

Take ten minutes today and be bone-deep honest with God about who you truly are, not who you hope to be. Receive his lightly held mercy. And having experienced God's grace in the face of your flaws, go and do the same for others. Accept each person in each interaction today as they are, not as you wish they were.

23

Treating Your Hurry Sickness

The Role of Relationships

If you can't get along with others, you can't get along in the world. This is a rigid reality. Success in any sphere of life requires interacting successfully with other people. Many multitalented people have failed to achieve their goals or their potential because they simply stunk at connecting with others. As much as we'd like to fantasize that we could get our way if people would just stay out of our way, there's no way this is going to happen. This is especially true when considering our life under God. We cannot answer the question, "How am I doing in my religion?" without answering the question, "How am I doing in my relationships?"

Jesus demonstrates the critical nature of human connections by making them one of the three main topics in his Sermon on the Mount. He implies that on the dashboard of human life, the quality of our relationships is one of three gauges we are to watch. Spiritual health and vitality are measured by this gauge. The journey to the top of his Mount is not a solo climb. It requires contact and communication with others.

James Bryan Smith writes that our interactions with humans are the frontline of the spiritual life: "Our daily encounters with others are the arenas in which our relationship with God becomes incarnate."[21] Relationships, from strangers to soulmates, are where we put the "walk" into our "talk." The ultimate test of the authenticity of your faith is how you act toward the next person you see: the busy mail carrier at your mailbox, the distracted teen taking your order at the drive through, the cranky coworker in the cubicle next to yours, or the weary woman who greets you at day's end.

Hurry Sickness

Many of our daily interactions suffer from a debilitating illness. This disease clouds our eyes—we seldom seem to even see the people around us. It clogs our heart—we frequently fail to feel compassion for those near us. And it cripples our hands—we regularly neglect to lend a hand to those in need.

What is this malady? Author John Ortberg calls it "hurry sickness."[22] It's also known as busyness or hurriedness. Simply put, our fast-paced living undermines most of our attempts at Christlike loving. It's nearly impossible to truly see others, genuinely support others, and authentically serve others when we are going ninety-miles-per-hour through life. Love withers in the heat of hurry.

We seem to be in an awfully big hurry. A survey of over twenty thousand Christians in more than one hundred countries found that 40 percent of us say we "often" or "always" rush from task to task.[23] Sadly, this number was even higher for church ministers (54 percent).

But most of us probably don't need a survey to help us spot this sickness in ourselves. We can feel it in our bones. A quick review of our day reveals that many of us exhibit one or more symptoms of hurry sickness:[24]

- Speeding – Because we are plagued by fear that there are too many to-do's and too few tick-tocks, we read faster, talk faster, drive faster, and work faster. Despite increased speed, however, we do not typically experience increased productivity.

- Multitasking – While driving we're also drinking, eating, and phoning. While we watch television we do homework and send text messages. Doing one thing at a time seems like such a waste of time.

- Clutter – We have multiple to-do lists, stacks of unread magazines, and tons of unfinished projects. There's not enough time to straighten up each area of our life, thus we straighten up little to nothing.

- Superficiality – We do not have the time to develop deep character or create deep relationships. As a result, we settle for the superficial.

- Lovelessness – Ortberg writes, "The most serious sign of hurry sickness is a diminished capacity to love. Love and hurry are fundamentally incompatible. Love always takes time, and time is one thing hurried people don't have."[25]
- Sunset Fatigue – When we come home at the end of the day, we're at the end of our rope. Our emotional tank is empty, and we have no fuel left to invest in the people or the projects most in need of our energy.

One of the things that most hinders our ability to lean into Jesus' vision for the relationships in our lives is the rush of our lives. We simply don't have time for people. If we wish to experience Jesus' dream for human connections, hurry must be eliminated at all cost. "Slowing" is the name given to any habit or effort undertaken with this goal in mind. It consists of any intentional effort to reduce speed in order to increase love.

Mark Buchanan tells of an anti-speeding campaign in British Columbia, Canada.[26] There were large billboards placed in prominent places along major roads, showing black-and-white photos of terrible car wrecks. Underneath the photos were these words: "Speed is killing us. Slow down and live." We might put it another way: "Speed is killing us. Slow down and love."

TAKE ⑩

Take ten minutes today and score yourself (1–5) on each of the symptoms of hurry sickness: speeding, multitasking, clutter, superficiality, lovelessness, and sunset fatigue. Here's your scoring range: 1 = no trace of this symptom in my life; 2 = small and somewhat rare traces of this symptom in my life; 3 = medium and irregular traces of this symptom in my life; 4 = medium and regular traces of this symptom in my life; 5 = this symptom looms large in my life and is always present). What's your score? Are you surprised?

Now, complete this sentence: One way I can slow down and decrease my hurry sickness is _____.

24

Growing by Slowing

Breaking the Growth Barrier

Mike Yaconelli offers these challenging words about a prominent barrier to spiritual growth:

> What keeps many of us from growing is not sin but speed... Spiritual growth is not running faster, as in more meetings, more Bible studies, and more prayer meetings. Spiritual growth happens when we slow our activity down. If we want to meet Jesus, we can't do it on the run. If we want to stay on the road of faith, we have to hit the brakes, pull over to a rest area, and stop. Christianity is not about inviting Jesus to speed through life with us; it's about noticing Jesus at the rest stop.[27]

To remain on the road of faith, we have to hit the brakes. Deceleration is especially necessary for healthy relationships. For many of us, it was our failure to brake that ultimately created brokenness in a relationship. When we survey the moments in which we've most harmed or neglected others, many of them correlate with times of hurry. The greater the hurry, the greater the harm. What keeps many of us from growing, especially in our capacity for love, is not merely the selfishness of our hearts but the speed of our lives. If we want to break our greatest growth barrier, we're going to have to stop trying to break the speed barrier.

We cannot be who Jesus envisioned us to be in relationship to other people when rushing characterizes our lives. Relationships take time. Compassion takes time. Kindness takes time. The more we bring hurry in our encounters with others the less we bring help. The greater our busyness around others, the fewer blessings we bring to them.

The cure? Slow down. Joseph Bailey suggests that love has a certain speed; it travels at a certain rate. What is that speed? Bailey argues that love usually travels much slower than we do. If we wish to practice more love, we have to reduce our RPMs so that we are traveling at the speed of love.[28] This allows us to be fully present in any given moment—present to those around us and sensitive to their needs.

A friend of mine is one of those multitalented people for whom doors of opportunity always seem to open. He's been offered several promotions at work, but he's turned down most of them. He's refused the invitation to climb another rung on the ladder of success. Why? He put it this way: "I realized that saying 'Yes' to that promotion was saying 'Yes' to more duties at work and less time at home. I just couldn't do that to myself or my family." He made a conscious decision to slow. And his family has reaped the rewards.

What's your current speed? How does this differ from the speed of love?

Steps to Slowing

Slowing is a discipline designed to eradicate frenzy from our lives. The practice of slowing involves intentionally placing yourself in circumstances that create time for noticing and attending to others. Slowing means placing yourself in a situation where you are forced to wait.

Here are some small ways to start practicing slowing:[29]

- On your way home, drive your car in the slow lane; this forces you to reduce your pace and create space for considering how you might bless those awaiting your arrival at home.
- Eat your food slowly.
- Get in the longest line at the grocery store.
- Go the entire day without looking at a clock.
- Don't schedule back-to-back appointments with no break in between.
- Take a deep breath before answering the phone.

These practices only prompt growth if we are intentional within them. We are not just creating time to kill, but also time to contribute. As we slow down, we strive to become attentive to our surroundings and to the Spirit. We seek to remember that God is present in each moment and that he may wish to use us to bless someone nearby.

TAKE ⑩

Take ten minutes today and force yourself into a situation in which you have to wait. While your engine idles, look around. Who do you see? Can you tell what they need? In what ways might God work through you to bless them? Take a moment and silently pray for God to use this "idle" time to bless someone.

25

The Ministry of Marinating

"You are the salt of the earth" (Mt. 5:13a).

Salt adds flavor. Salt provides variety. But, above all, in the ancient world, salt prevented decay. It kept perishables from perishing. And in his Sermon on the Mount, Jesus imagines that we can be salt in the lives of others. He believes God can use us to prevent emotional, psychological, and spiritual decay in peoples' lives. As salt, we can be agents of preservation and conservation.

"You are the light of the world" (Mt. 5:14a).

Light illumines. Light warms. Light encourages. And in his Sermon on the Mount, Jesus sees us acting as light in the lives of others. He believes God can use us to provide hope, warmth, and vision in peoples' lives. As light, we can be agents of illumination and inspiration.

These images of salt and light summarize the sky-high view Jesus has of the impact we can make in human interactions. God has made us capable of radically impacting people for good.

One thing, however, keeps this dream from even getting off the ground—hurry. Because we rush from one activity to another, our salt rarely has sufficient time to contact others long enough to keep their decay at bay. Our light rarely has sufficient time to enlighten others long enough to drive their darkness away. Though we may be quite salty and shiny, we're on the move so much that the salt and light can't do their work. We're like a crazed man sprinting through a cafeteria where people sit with trays of bland food. While he runs to them and then past them, he sprinkles salt all around him hoping that some of it will land on the food. Or we're like a frantic woman speeding through an office area where the power has gone out pointing our flashlight at a full sprint, expecting office workers to understand what we are doing, get up out of their chairs, and run after us.

What's needed is some way to decelerate long enough for our saltiness to actually contact and impact the people around us. What's required is some method of slowing so our shine can fully saturate the people near us. When we imagine acting as salt, we may wish to imagine something akin to marinating. When we envision acting as light, we may wish to picture something like tanning. Both require time in order to have their full impact. To be effective, we need the spiritual habit of slowing, which is designed to reduce hurry and enlarge our potential for being salt and light in the life of each person we contact during the day.

Slowing and Simplicity

Slowing is related to another spiritual habit that we'll explore later–simplicity. As he explores the life of Jesus, Gary Holloway relates that Jesus not only had a simplified exterior life but a simplified interior life as well. He writes, "Jesus knew he had his limits. He could not do it all. He did not heal everyone, teach everyone, or worry over everyone. Instead he had a single heart that focused on the calling and mission he had from God."[30] Slowing grows out of an ability to streamline our goals, dreams, and purposes in life. Rather than trying to get a hundred things done, we try to get a handful done. This leaves us plenty of margin–flex-space in our lives to respond to people as we come across them. Such simplicity comes from having a single-hearted focus on God and only doing what we believe he has called us to do. When God's to-do list is the only thing we say "Yes" to, there is always enough time to complete it. We do not strive to do everything or help everyone. We strive only to do the limited things we truly believe God has called us to.

Thus slowing begins by simplifying our aspirations and our goals. When we limit the number of projects and people we are attempting to attend to, we increase our ability to truly slow down and become more effective and fruitful.

Slowing and Sabbath

This type of simplification is a type of Sabbath. Sabbath is spending a day or a portion of a day resting with God. This may seem radical to some because we cannot imagine setting work aside for an entire day. We begin to worry about all the work that is not getting done. Thus, in Sabbath "we truly rest from our work by letting God take care of things. For one day, we let him do our work for us."[31]

Sabbath centers on ceasing all work and trusting God to take care of the world without us and our work.

Slowing is Sabbath in miniature. We cease certain aspects of our work—limiting ourselves to only doing certain projects and tasks—and we trust that God will accomplish whatever else is truly important. This reduction in work allows us to reduce our pace and become more available to God and to others around us. Slowing and Sabbath have the same core theology: God can run the world without us, and he does not need us to run ragged in order to keep the world spinning. So, we slow. We leave some items off the to-do list in order to create space and presence for others.

TAKE ⑩

Take ten minutes today to identify one thing you do not have to do today because you trust that God is still capable of running the world without your help. Identify just one thing that can wait for another day or another week to get done. Now, in the space created by eliminating that one thing, breathe. Rest. Be present to God and to whomever happens to be near you at the time. Use this space to contribute in a meaningful way to that person.

26

Shifting Your Center of Gravity

A Passion for People Begins in Prayer

When Jesus closes his eyes and imagines the way his followers would interact with others on earth, what does he see? He sees relationships in which we do not react in anger toward those who discourage or disappoint us (Mt. 5:21–22). He envisions collaborations in which we resolve conflict quickly (Mt. 5:23–26). He imagines people who turn their cheeks and go the second mile (Mt. 5:38–41). He visualizes a community filled with people who love their enemies and pray for those who make life difficult (Mt. 5:43–48). He pictures followers who forgive others in the same way God has forgiven them (Mt. 6:12).

When you close your eyes and visualize the way you've been interacting with others, is this what you see? Do your relationships reflect Jesus' revelation?

Jesus wants us to be passionate for life-changing connections with others. Christianity is not just between you and God. It's between you, God, and each living person you contact. Jesus summarized the main message of Scripture in this way: love God and love people. Following Christ is a two-love lifestyle. Passion for God must be accompanied by passion for people. And this passion for people can be sparked and fueled by prayer for people. It's a basic principle: the more frequently we pray for people with our lips, the more likely we'll be to love them with our lives. It becomes increasingly difficult to ignore or injure a person for whom we've also been interceding.

If petition is prayer dedicated to the issues in my own life, then intercession is prayer dedicated to the issues in the lives of others. And as we shift our prayer life from petition-only to intercession-also, we are "shifting our center of gravity from our own needs to the needs and concerns of others."[32] Intercessory prayer is one of the primary ways to prioritize and prize the people in our lives.

Intercession is, as Marjorie Thompson explains, the most "concrete expression of the social dimension of prayer."[33] Jesus' vision in his Sermon on the Mount is a social vision—it is a dream about the connections between people. Jesus does not imagine us as isolated individuals living in intimacy with God. He imagines us as connected community—a society—living in intimacy with others and with God. Intercession puts flesh on this social vision. It is one of the many incarnations of kindness and compassion.

American Quaker theologian Douglas Steere pushes this concept even further. He contends, "Intercession is the most intensely social act that the human being is capable of."[34] It's not drilling water wells or serving at a rescue mission or bringing a meal over to someone in need. As good as these things are, they are not the most intensely social act we are capable of. What is? Intercessory prayer. If you are searching for the supreme way to serve people, put your knees on the floor and their names on your lips. Love may lead to things beyond this, but love begins with intercessory prayer. Richard Foster explains, "If we truly love people, we will desire for them far more than it is within our power to give them, and this will lead us to prayer. Intercession is a way of loving others."[35] If you are a parent, consider all the great things you desire for your children. Deep spirituality. Supportive friends. A meaningful education. A thriving career. If you have a close friend, reflect on the many significant things you aspire for that person. Success in the workplace. Courageous faith. Opportunities to make a difference. Freedom from evil. We desire and seek the sort of things for loved ones we are incapable of supplying. And because we often desire far more for them than we can deliver, the best gift we can grant them is the gift of intercession.

A Way to Intercede

Over the years, my intercessions have taken many forms. For the last five years, I've followed a disciplined plan that allows me to intercede for more people in more significant ways. Here's how I organize my weekly intercession:

DAILY	There are some intercessory prayers I engage in every day. These include specific prayers for my wife, children, and extended family members.
Monday	Intercession for each staff member and elder in my congregation.
Tuesday	Intercession for those recently baptized in my congregation and those who are new members in my congregation.
Wednesday	Intercession for specific missionaries within and without the United States.
Thursday	Intercession for specific friends and colleagues.
Friday	Intercession for individuals whom I call "kingdom leaders"—ministers, directors of charities, lay leaders, staff and administration at colleges/universities, etc.
Saturday	Individuals who've requested prayer during the week.
Sunday	Individuals who've requested prayer during the week.

There are, of course, many ways to intercede. A friend of mine keeps a running log of people who ask for prayers and then prays through that list day after day after day. Another friend keeps a three-ring binder with pictures of the people she prays for regularly. She gazes at each picture as she intercedes for each person. Still another friend likes to physically go into the room of each family member when the house is empty and intercede for them. The important thing is to find a way to record and/or remember the people in your life who need your prayers and to pray regularly for them.

TAKE ⑩

Take ten minutes today to begin a list of people for whom you can intercede. Now, intercede.

27

Packing Your Prayer Closet

During her sunset years of life, Kendra's grandmother hand-stitched several colorful quilts for Kendra, my wife. They are some of our favorite heirlooms, especially the double wedding band quilt. The blankets remind us of Memaw's generous love, fun-loving spirit, and quirky personality.

Perhaps you have an heirloom from a much-loved one. A family piano. A treasured set of crystal. A piece of framed art. These items reflect that individual's kindness and care. They tell us something about the heart of that person.

Leaving an inheritance is a common practice. We've come to expect it from those who are important to us. But what about the One who is most important? Did Jesus leave an heirloom? If so, what was it? What gift did Jesus bequeath to those who lived after he left? If Jesus had written a will, what legacy would he have listed on its pages?

Perhaps with such questions in mind, George Buttrick writes this: "Two signs of Jesus abide, though all else be ignored or forgotten—a prayer and a cross… These are His memorial: not a tombstone or a moneyed foundation, but a simple prayer and a gallows set against the daybreak."[36]

The Heirloom of Prayer

You may not be surprised to find the cross listed on Jesus' Last Will and Testament. Almost universally, when people think of the Christ, they think of the cross. The worldwide symbol of Jesus' contribution to humanity is the symbol of his death. It is also the world-changing summary of Jesus' challenge to humanity. He died so we might live. As his followers, we die so that others might live.

But you may be surprised by Buttrick's mention of a prayer as part of Jesus' memorial. A prayer is listed among his most prized possessions? Yes, and the prayer Buttrick is referring to is what we call the "Lord's Prayer." Besides the cross, what captures the heart of Jesus is the heirloom bequeathed to us in his Lord's Prayer. As Jesus sought some way to pass down what most mattered to him, he chose to grant us the inheritance of Calvary's cross and the Lord's Prayer. William Willimon and Stanley Hauerwas write, "So if you are asked, 'Who is a Christian?' the best answer you can give is, 'A Christian is none other than someone who has learned to pray the Lord's Prayer.'"[37] To be a Christian is to pray Jesus' prayer.

What's so valuable about this prayer? Consider its wonderful words:

Pray then like this:

"Our Father in heaven,
  hallowed be your name.
Your kingdom come,
your will be done,
  on earth as it is in heaven.
Give us this day our daily bread,
and forgive us our debts,
  as we also have forgiven our debtors.
And lead us not into temptation,
  but deliver us from evil." (Mt. 6:9–13)

This prayer, as Frederick Buechner notes, focuses primarily on God's omnipotence and our impotence. It is rooted in the belief that God can still do anything and that we still can't do much of anything. It is the ultimate declaration of dependence. It puts God in his place, while it puts us in ours.

We do well not to pray the prayer lightly. It takes guts to pray it at all... "Thy will be done" is what we are saying. That is the climax of the first half of the prayer. We are asking God to be God. We are asking God to do not what we want but what God wants... To speak those words is to invite the tiger out of the cage, to unleash a power that makes atomic power look like a warm breeze. You need to be bold in another way to speak the second half. Give us. Forgive us. Don't test us. Deliver us. If it takes guts to face the omnipotence that is God's, it takes perhaps not less to face the impotence that is ours. We can do nothing without God. Without God we are nothing.[38]

Authors Mike Breem and Steve Cockram propose that everything Jesus taught about life in the kingdom of God is summarized in this brief prayer. In other words, to live as Jesus wants is to live out this prayer. This is true discipleship, and it comes only as we learn to pray this prayer.[39]

The cross and this prayer. These are Jesus' greatest gifts. In them we find all that is needed for a life of following in his footsteps.

The Lord's Prayer as Intercession

One of the reasons for the importance of the Lord's Prayer is the intercession modeled within it. The prayer begins with three lines of surrender. These lines are focused upon God–hallowed be your name; your kingdom come; your will be done. These are followed by four lines of supplication, which are focused upon ourselves–daily bread, forgiveness, no temptation, deliverance from the evil one. The intercessory nature of the prayer is seen in its use of first person plural in both the lines of surrender and the lines of supplication: "Our Father in heaven… Give us this day our daily bread, and forgive us our debts… And lead us not into temptation, but deliver us from evil." This is not a prayer just for "me." It is a prayer for "we." This is not just a prayer for my necessities. It is a prayer for our necessities. This is a prayer prayed on behalf of others, not just ourselves.

The intercessory nature of the prayer begins with its very first phrase: "Our Father." David Buttrick writes,

> If we pray the prayer, we must reach out to the world, knowing that everyone is a child of God no matter what their nationality, faith, language, skin color, or sexual orientation. God claims us all as family, even those heirs who may have misplaced their religious birth certificates. The "our" in "our Father"…acknowledges that we cannot stand alone before God. We must stand with our neighbors. "Our Father" forces us to join the human family.[40]

The door into this prayer is the widest possible door. It allows me to enter the prayer closet bringing, not only myself, but my family, my neighbors, my boss, my waiter, the victim of a gunshot from another state featured on last night's news, and the refugees fleeing their country who appeared in last week's periodicals. My prayer closet is packed to standing room only with the faces and names of the many for whom I am now privileged to intercede. I enter the Lord's Prayer praying for the millions included in the word *our*.

What do we pray for these countless members of the human family? While we could pray many things, Jesus identifies four items:

1. "Give *us* this day *our* daily bread." We ask that others in our village, city, nation, and world would have the physical resources needed to survive and thrive today.
2. "Forgive *us our* debts, as *we* forgive *our* debtors." We beg that others across the street and across the ocean would have the sins removed that stand between them and God, and that they would in turn remove the sins standing between them and others.
3. "Lead *us* not into temptation." We request that coworkers at the office and co-inhabitants of the planet would not have to endure times of trial, testing, or suffering.
4. "Deliver *us* from evil." We beg God to protect neighbors and nations from the one who seeks their ultimate downfall.

TAKE ⑩

Take ten minutes today and pray the second half of the Lord's Prayer on behalf of a specific list of individuals: "Father, I come to you on behalf of _____. Please grant _____ the physical resources he/she needs to survive and thrive. Please forgive _____ for any sins that stand between him/her and you. Please help _____ to forgive others who may have done unkind things to him/her. Please keep _____ from times of trial, testing, or suffering. And please protect _____ from the evil one."

28

The Greatest Need of Others

Pastor Gordon MacDonald recalls his time at Ground Zero following 9/11.[41] Amidst the debris, dust, and dedicated rescuers, MacDonald had come to deliver whatever pastoral aid he could. There he met a Trappist monk who wore a brown robe fastened with a white rope. As MacDonald shadowed his new friend through the mayhem, person after person made their way to the monk because they wanted prayer. "Will you bless me?" they asked over and over. The monk would lay his hands on their sooty heads and pray, "May the peace of God and the love of Jesus and the strength of the Holy Spirit be upon you."

At the bottom of one of the deepest pits in U. S. history, what victims most wanted was prayer. When they felt the curse of a broken world most deeply, what they wished for most desperately was someone who could ask for the blessings of God. They needed someone who could stand before the Father and intercede on their behalf.

MacDonald also tells of John Frederick Oberlin. Oberlin ministered to impoverished parishioners in France in the nineteenth century. Each morning between nine and ten Oberlin prayed for the people of the valley. Residents came to so prize his prayers that they established a rule–no one who passed by Oberlin's home during his hour of prayer was permitted to make noise. Nothing was to distract him from his intercessions. The people believed the quality of their lives depended on the quality of his prayers.

There are few things as cherished and crucial as intercessory prayer. It not only allows the one praying to express care for others in concrete ways, but it allows the hurting and needy to find a measure of comfort. Nothing consoles like the knowledge that someone is praying on your behalf.

How then, can we grow in our own ministry of intercessory prayer? Here are three nontraditional ways to practice intercession.

Intercession as Listening

Richard Foster proposes that intercession starts with listening:[42] "Listening to the Lord is the first thing, the second thing, and the third thing necessary for successful intercession." For example, he suggests, instead of continuing to pray for Aunt Susie's arthritis just as you have been for twenty years, stop and listen. Perhaps God wishes you to pray for something else, something deeper, something of even greater need for Aunt Susie. Talking to God on behalf of a person must always begin by listening to God about that person.

Think of one individual in your life right now. In your mind, see that individual. Now sit quietly before God with that individual in your heart. What does he or she truly need? What is most urgent for that person? Now, let that be the focus of your prayer.

Intercession as Flash Prayers

Foster also suggests that intercession can take the form of "flash prayers"–praying short and silent prayers for each person we see and interact with during the day.[43] This type of on-going intercession may, in fact, be the most personally transformative type of prayer. It not only impacts those we pray for, but it changes us because it forces our minds to be focused on others rather than on ourselves throughout the day. Dallas Willard says, "[P]rayer as a discipline has its greatest force in strengthening the spiritual life only as we learn to pray without ceasing (1 Thess. 5:17; Phil. 4:6)."[44] Flash prayers allow us to engage in a kind of incessant intercession.

If you have the opportunity to be among a group of people today at work, at school, in a store, or in your neighborhood, intercede silently for every individual you see. As you walk, shop, talk, or do business, pray for each person.

Intercession as Countercultural Action

Jesus teaches important issues about intercession in his Lord's Prayer. But he also speaks about intercession elsewhere in the Sermon on the Mount: "You have heard that it was said, 'You shall love your neighbor and hate your enemy.' But I say to you, Love your enemies and pray for those who persecute you, so that you may be sons of your Father who is in heaven." (Mt. 5:43–45a, emphasis added)

Conventional wisdom, Jesus says, urges us to love those who love us (e.g., our neighbor) and hate those who hate us. The norm is to do unto others as they've done unto us. Yet Jesus is building a countercultural community. We are called not only to display kindness and compassion in the face of those who adore us, but also in the face of those who abhor us. We are to love even our enemies, even those who are the source of our deepest wounds. And what concrete form is our unexpected esteem to take? Intercession. Jesus says, "Love your enemies and pray for those who persecute you." Jesus can think of no greater expression of genuine concern for the antagonists in our lives than intercessory prayer.

It's important to recognize that the phrase "and pray for those who persecute you" does not refer to imprecatory prayer. The Psalms are filled with examples of righteous people praying for their enemies–but praying for God to smite them! Jesus invites us, not to imprecatory prayer for our enemies, but to intercessory prayer. It's the difference between, "Bash them, God!" and, "Bless them, God!"

Think right now about someone who has hurt you: a spouse, a child, a parent, a former friend, a coworker, or a classmate. Now, pray positively for that person. If you can't think of anyone who has hurt you recently, James Bryan Smith suggests this: pray for a competitor. Specifically, pray for the success of a competitor.[45] Change the adversarial relationship of the marketplace to one of compassion and kindness.

TAKE ⑩

Take ten minutes today to practice one of these three forms of intercession.

SECTION FOUR

Generous with Possessions

29

Dodging the Dark Side

There's a moment, I'm told, when a minister goes from preachin' to meddlin'. When a minister moves from scratching itching ears to stepping on sensitive toes. For better or worse, Jesus and we have reached that moment. Elsewhere in his Sermon on the Mount, Jesus has pressed us into more authentic relationships with others and a more genuine relationship with God. But halfway through chapter 6, Jesus begins spelling out the painful and practical implications of all of this in terms of one thing: money. He reveals that our life in the kingdom will have consequences related to our cash and credit cards.

Jesus teaches us not to be miserly and serve "Money." Rather, we are to be generous and serve God (Mt. 6:19-24). He issues a challenging call for us to consider which one we are truly serving and what it might mean to live more generously. In addition, Jesus urges us not to get stressed over stuff. Rather, we are to trust in the caring provision and kingdom purpose of God (vv. 25-34). This section demands an honest look at our wealth worries and what it could look like to believe "In God we trust" instead of "In treasures we trust."

Jesus uses these two teachings to show that the way we deal with our finances can be a significant way in which we bless our Father and our friends. Some of the principal expressions of our piety and our concern for people will come through the use of our possessions. An important indication of the quality of our connection to God and our relations with others is how we're using our income.

The Dark Side of Possessions

There is both a "dark side" and a "light side" to possessions.[1] God issues warnings and outlines dangers associated with wealth and riches. But he also reveals blessings and opportunities that arise from treasures and goods.

The dark side can be seen in Scriptures such as the following:

- "Do not lay up for yourselves treasures on earth, where moth and rust destroy and where thieves break in and steal, but lay up for yourselves treasures in heaven, where neither moth nor rust destroys, and where thieves do not break in and steal... No one can serve two masters, for either he will hate the one and love the other, or he will be devoted to the one and despise the other. You cannot serve both God and money." (Mt. 6:19-20, 24)
- "Again I tell you, it is easier for a camel to go through the eye of a needle than for a rich person to enter the kingdom of God." (Mt. 19:24)
- "Those who want to get rich fall into temptation and a trap and into many foolish and harmful desires that plunge people into ruin and destruction. For the love of money is a root of all kinds of evil. Some people, eager for money, have wandered from the faith and pierced themselves with many griefs." (1 Tim. 6:9-10, NIV)
- "Now listen, you rich people, weep and wail because of the misery that is coming on you. Your wealth has rotted, and moths have eaten your clothes. Your gold and silver are corroded. Their corrosion will testify against you and eat your flesh like fire. You have hoarded wealth in the last days. Look! The wages you failed to pay the workers who mowed your fields are crying out against you. The cries of the harvesters have reached the ears of the Lord Almighty. You have lived on earth in luxury and self-indulgence. You have fattened yourselves in the day of slaughter. You have condemned and murdered the innocent one, who was not opposing you." (Jas. 5:1-6, NIV)

Possessions have the power to become the primary competitor to God in your life. Of all that might distract us from God, money is at the top of the list. Because of this, it is difficult for people of means to truly live under God's rule. In the end, many of us will wind up placing our faith in things that will rot, rust, and be stolen.

The Light Side of Possessions

Yet Scripture is also filled with stories of people granted many means by God and wielding wealth for the sake of God and others:

- After this, Jesus traveled about from one town and village to another, proclaiming the good news of the kingdom of God. The Twelve were with him, and also some women who had been cured of evil spirits and diseases: Mary (called Magdalene) from whom seven demons had come out; Joanna the wife of Chuza, the manager of Herod's household; Susanna; and many others. These women were helping to support them out of their own means. (Lk. 8:1–3, NIV)
- Joseph, a Levite from Cyprus, whom the apostles called Barnabas (which means 'son of encouragement'), sold a field he owned and brought the money and put it at the apostles' feet. (Acts 4:36–37, NIV)
- You will be enriched in every way so that you can be generous on every occasion, and through us your generosity will result in thanksgiving to God. (2 Cor. 9:11, NIV)
- Command those who are rich in this present world not to be arrogant nor to put their hope in wealth, which is so uncertain, but to put their hope in God, who richly provides us with everything for our enjoyment. Command them to do good, to be rich in good deeds, and to be generous and willing to share. In this way they will lay up treasure for themselves as a firm foundation for the coming age, so that they may take hold of the life that is truly life. (1 Tim. 6:17–19, NIV)

The finances of certain women underwrote Jesus' ministry. The generosity of the Corinthians supplied the need of others. The treasures of many enabled them to be rich in good deeds. Your wealth is a gift given by God to you for others. He grants you the great joy of participating in the gift giving. Goods can be leveraged to bless God and those around us in a myriad of ways.

Practicing Hospitality

One simple discipline that empowers us to use resources rather than be used by them is hospitality. Adele Calhoun defines hospitality in this way: "to be a safe person who offers others the grace, shelter and presence of Jesus."[2] Hospitality is not simply offering a place to stay the night, providing a good meal with some good conversation, or giving someone a ride home from an event. It's the offer of these things so that a person might experience through them the grace, shelter, and presence of Jesus. Our goal is to allow others to enjoy Jesus' hospitality through our own. We take all that we own and offer it for Jesus' use in making others feel welcomed, included, and valued.

I gained my first and fullest glimpse of hospitality in the cozy home of my teacher and coach Don Warren. Coach Warren spent twenty-eight years investing in young people in the classroom and on the playing field. The majority of his coaching efforts were poured into shaping the boys basketball programs in Dexter and Cloudcroft, New Mexico. He won twelve district championships, four regional championships, and had four top-four finishes in the New Mexico state tournament. Coach Warren was named his district's coach of the year eleven times, and earned the 1987 New Mexico Coach of the Year award. In 1997 he was inducted into the New Mexico High School Coaches Association Hall of Honor.

Coach Warren influenced me in the small classrooms of Cloudcroft High (twenty-six in my graduating class) and on the basketball court and football field of our single A school (the smallest designation in New Mexico athletics). But perhaps his longest-lasting influence on me came from the gatherings he hosted in his home after the games.

Coach Warren and his wife Judy, together with their daughters Leah and Michal, invited players, coaches, and referees to their house after most home games. Winter hats and letter jackets were piled on a bed, couches and kitchen chairs were rearranged, and athletes and adults mingled, snacked, and laughed as the games' bloopers were verbally replayed. Everyone was welcome–opposing coaches, helpful and hurtful referees, stars who never left the game, and subs who never left the bench. As a teenager, it was a safe place where people were always glad to see me arrive and sad to see me go. And, in a town so small it didn't even have a stoplight, it was the best (and only) nightlife around. Coach Warren's is still the face I picture and the home I envision when I think of hospitality.

It's the kind of thing Jesus envisions for all of us–loving God and loving neighbor through warm and gracious hospitality. He calls us to use things such as a meal, money, or a few moments of time to show people we're immensely glad to see them.

TAKE ⑩

Take ten minutes today to use something you own in an act of hospitality for another person.

30

Spreading Good News by Sharing Good Food

Possessing, Using, or Trusting?

My family and I have moved four times. Each time, I'm amazed at how much stuff we own. The number of boxes it takes to package our possessions increases immensely with every relocation. The size of the truck it takes to transport our treasures expands enormously with each transition. At times, it leaves me wondering if the things I possess are starting to possess me.

I've found Dallas Willard's writings helpful in my working through this challenge. He articulates the difference between possessing riches, using riches, and trusting in riches.[3]

- To *possess* riches is to have the right to say how they will or will not be used. Possession is a neutral matter. Possessing riches can be good or bad. It is simply having the authority to determine how something will or will not be handled.
- To *use* riches is to cause them to be consumed or transferred to others in exchange for something we desire. Where possession merely indicates having a right to say how something will be used, use indicates actually taking that resource and using it for something we desire.
- Finally, to *trust* in riches is to count upon them to obtain or secure that which we truly treasure. It is to think that riches will bring us happiness, well-being, and security.

Our problems with wealth tend to revolve around the mis-*use* of and mis-*trust* in riches. The Bible does not condemn the *possession* of riches outright. There is nothing necessarily wrong or right with the *possession* of wealth. Challenges (and sins) arise when those with resources *use* what is in their possession for their own gain, or begin to *trust* in riches as the pathway to satisfaction in life.

Trust is a particularly bothersome issue. Trust in treasures is a transgression affecting both those living with plenty and those living in poverty. I have known homeless mothers plagued with the conviction that security and happiness could only come through the home, job, or retirement plan that they didn't yet possess. And I have known company presidents deceived by the belief that security and happiness were grounded in the home, job, and retirement plan they already possessed.

Possession of resources becomes a vice when it is paired with trust in riches and the use of them for selfish purposes. But that same possession becomes a virtue when paired with trust in God and the use of riches for God's purposes. I think of a local doctor who takes a team each year to serve in a medical clinic for the poor in Guatemala, the CEO who funds multiple ministries in Memphis, and the entrepreneur in Dallas who has poured tens of thousands of dollars into helping new churches start and thrive. Though wealthy, these individuals have found ways to use their assets for others and for God.

Hospitality as Gospel

Whether you have a lot or a little, hospitality enables you to do something similar. Hospitality empowers the moneyed and the meager to use goods for the good of others and the glory of God. Henri Nouwen identifies it as one of the most important customs for followers of Jesus to recover: "If there is any concept worth restoring to its original depth and evocative potential, it is the concept of hospitality."[4] In fact, theologian and ethicist Christine Pohl finds that for centuries hospitality was responsible for much of the spreadability and credibility of the gospel.[5] Christians stood out because they not only welcomed friends, family, and those with the means to repay, but also embraced the sick, the poor, and those without the ability to reciprocate. In addition, Christians regularly received those whom others rejected, especially those of different moral, ethnic, and social backgrounds. Hospitality thus offered Christians a design for sharing the gospel with their lives and a doorway for sharing the gospel with their lips.

Practicing Hospitality

Marjorie Thompson defines hospitality in this way: "Hospitality means receiving the other, from the heart, into my own dwelling place. It entails providing for the need, comfort, and delight of the other with all the openness, respect, freedom, tenderness, and joy that love itself embodies."[6] The "other," she explains, can be any person, but should include enemies and strangers. The "dwelling place" can be a physical space, such as a room, apartment, or house, or it can be an emotional or mental space–inviting others into the inner world of our thoughts and feelings, and giving people "room" to be heard and understood. Traditionally, Thompson says, hospitality provides food and drink, shelter and rest, protection and care, enjoyment and peace for others. She describes five forms of hospitality:[7]

1. Hospitality at *home* means parents being genuinely present to their children and making the home a place where mistakes can be made and forgiveness can be granted. Hospitality at home can also include adoption of hard-to-place children, sheltering a homeless couple, or taking in a foreign student.
2. Hospitality in the *workplace* involves listening to others' ideas, concerns, and critiques. It means creating a welcoming and inviting environment for coworkers, supervisors, and customers.
3. Hospitality in the *neighborhood* can be expressed by watching a neighbor's home or pets when they are away, listening to a lonely neighbor, watching the kids of a single parent in the neighborhood, or throwing a block party for neighbors.
4. Hospitality in our *churches* takes place when we welcome visitors and newcomers, honor each member's gifts, deal appropriately with conflict, intercede for others, and treat church staff generously.
5. Finally, *civic* hospitality involves creating schools, and providing medical care and recreation available to all; welcoming immigrants, the poor, and the undereducated into our communities; and treating the environment with care.

TAKE ⑩

Take ten minutes today and engage in an act of hospitality at home, in the workplace, in your neighborhood, in your church, or in the larger civic context in which you live.

31

Moving Like Jesus

As I write this chapter, the city of Memphis is awash with hospitality. The torrent began as a trickle in homes like mine. For example, asleep in our living room and guest room are three teens and a youth minister from another city. We've handed our beds, breakfasts, and bathrooms to them for five days. Hundreds of other homes in the mid-South are filled with similar company. These houseguests will pay forward our hospitality to others in massive amounts. Each day this week they will spill out across the city in teams and repair, restore, and repaint homes for the poor. It's called Memphis WorkCamp. Yesterday I spoke to the owner of one of the homes hit by this river of mercy. As she looked at the crew scraping, caulking, painting, and nailing, she told me how she'd been unable to do maintenance on her humble home for the last seven years. She said, "I prayed for God to send relief! And he did!" Since its beginnings twenty-four years ago, Memphis WorkCamp has poured out relief to nearly eight hundred homeowners. My family's gallon-sized act of hospitality for a work crew helped make possible this organization's gargantuan-sized act of hospitality for the poor. And all this hospitality was making Memphis one very happy and holy place.

The Priority of Hospitality

Perhaps this is why Henri Nouwen identified hospitality as one of three components central to the way of Christ.[8] Nouwen believed the spiritual life consisted of three aspects: our relationship with self, our connection to God, and our treatment of others. In each component, Nouwen taught that we must experience a certain "move" or transition. We will not be fulfilled or mature until this shift occurs in all three spaces of life.

First, when it comes to our interior life (the self), the most vital move is from loneliness to solitude. We switch from being lonely because we have no friends, to being alone because we seek companionship with God in the quiet. Second, in our fellowship with the Father, the crucial change is from illusion to prayer. We abandon the misconception that we are in control, and we seek through prayer to surrender to God's control. Third, regarding our union with others, the primary move is from hostility to hospitality. We repent of conflict and replace it with cordiality. We confess hatred and commit to hospitality.

Of the many indices we might consider for our spiritual life, Nouwen believed these three were most important. The maturity of our self will be decided by the measure of our solitude. The sincerity of our association with God will be established by the consistency of our prayers to God. And the depth of our love for neighbor is determined by the degree of our hospitality to neighbor.

In highlighting hospitality, Nouwen stood in solidarity with ancient followers of God. Biblical historian Rodney Duke writes of cordiality displayed by the Old Testament faithful.[9] Acts of hospitality included the welcoming of travelers into one's home for food, lodging, and protection (Gen. 18:2–8; 19:1–8; Job 31:16–23, 31–32), permitting the stranger to harvest the corners of ones fields (Lev. 19:9–10; Deut. 24:19–22; Ruth 2:2–17), clothing the naked (Isa. 58:7; Ezek. 18:7, 16), tithing food for the needy (Deut. 14:28–29; 26:1–11), and including the alien in religious celebrations (Ex. 12:48–49; Deut. 16:10–14). One of the greatest forms of hospitality was sharing a meal together. In the ancient world, to share a meal was to share life. Thus, God's meal with the elders of Israel (Ex. 24:1–11) was a marvelous act of hospitality.

Christine Pohl surveys the same spirit in the New Testament.[10] Early Christians demonstrated concrete expressions of care for sisters and brothers in the faith as well as for strangers, prisoners, and exiles. Their hospitality met physical and social needs in a way that communicated value for the person being served. Paul instructed believers to pursue hospitality (Rom. 12:13). The writer of the letter to the Hebrews urged Christians not to neglect it (Heb. 13:2). Peter challenged followers of Christ not to grumble about it (1 Pet. 4:9). Most importantly, Jesus modeled and mandated it (e.g., Lk. 14; Mt. 25). Pohl concludes that "Hospitality is not optional for Christians, nor is it limited to those who are specially gifted for it. It is, instead, a necessary practice in the community of faith."[11]

True and False Narratives

How, then, do we make this momentous move from hostility to hospitality? James Bryan Smith suggests it requires a change in narrative. We will have to rewrite some of the stories by which we live when it comes to our possessions.[12]

Smith finds that many of us base our approach to possessions on three false narratives:

1. First, we often live by the false narrative of *judgment*: "God helps those who help themselves." If this storyline is true, I am no longer required to help others through hospitality until they start helping themselves. Once they show some initiative in meeting their own needs, I'll finally fulfill some of those needs myself.

2. Second, we frequently live by the false narrative of *scarcity*: "If I give it away, I have less." If this plot is accurate, then I need to hold desperately to what I have for fear it will run out. I cannot share my meal with you because eventually there'll be no food left for either one of us.

3. Third, we regularly live by the false narrative of *entitlement*: "What I have is mine to use for my own pleasure." If this tale is true, I don't need to share with others because I worked hard for what I have and I deserve to enjoy it.

Smith argues that Jesus has come to alter these assumptions:

1. First, the false narrative of *judgment* ("God helps those who help themselves") will be edited into the true narrative of *helplessness*: "God helps those who cannot help themselves." Because I now believe there are people who cannot help themselves, I join God in alleviating their needs. Hospitality becomes one of the ways in which I do this.

2. Second, the false narrative of *scarcity* ("If I give it away, I have less") will be modified into the true narrative of *provision*: "If we all share, we all have enough." I now see myself as part of a community provisioned by God (whose resources have no end) and am thus able to give away what I have.

3. Third, the false narrative of *entitlement* ("What I have is mine to use for my own pleasure") is amended into the true narrative of *stewardship*: "What I have is God's to use for his glory." I may now use everything to bring honor and glory to God. A meal given, a bed offered, a conversation started, a jacket

shared, or a ride given to someone are now all opportunities to honor and glorify God.

False Narrative	True Narrative
Judgment: God helps those who help themselves.	Helplessness: God helps those who cannot help themselves.
Scarcity: If I give it away, I have less.	Provision: If we all share, we all have enough.
Entitlement: What I have is mine to use for my own pleasure.	Stewardship: What I have is God's to use for his glory.

TAKE ⑩

Take ten minutes today to identify which of the three false narratives above needs to be rewritten in your life. Invite the Holy Spirit to edit, rewrite, and rework the story by which you approach possessions. Ask the Spirit to empower you to make the move from hostility to hospitality.

32

Changing Your Focus

Eyes Ahead

My five-year-old daughter Jordan is in driving school this summer. Ok, she's not five. She's fifteen. But it was only yesterday that she was five. Now she's dating. And driving. It's surreal.

As Jordan and I have talked about her experiences in driving school, I've remembered something from my driver's education days. Vehicular instruction was offered by our high school and taught by one of our basketball coaches. I recall Coach Musgrove telling us, "Your car will go the direction you're looking." That's no longer true for me. I can look aside at a majestic mountain or a splendid sea while driving and not steer the car into it. But as a novice driver, this was very true. During my first times behind the wheel, when I focused on something to the right or left, my hands automatically steered to the right or left. Coach Musgrove had to keep telling me, "Eyes ahead. Eyes ahead."

A similar principal exists regarding possessions. Focus is imperative. For example, Jesus urges us to keep our "eye" centered upon things that lead to generosity rather than to greediness (Mt. 6:19–23). He asks us to "look" at how God provides the material needs of flowers and birds, and therefore to consider that God will provide for our needs as well (Mt. 6:25–30). He requests that we "seek" God's reign rather than godless riches (Mt. 6:33). "Eyes ahead," Jesus says. "Eyes ahead."

We need to do this because whatever captures our attention affects our direction. Jesus states, "Where your treasure is, there your heart will be also" (Mt. 6:21, NIV). Whatever we concentrate on, whatever we treasure, will become the dwelling place of our heart. The object of our eyes becomes the home of our heart. Look to the right or left at riches or resources, and your heart with its affections and loyalties will be steered in the same direction.

Our target not only affects the heart but our entire body. Jesus says, "If your eye is healthy, your whole body will be full of light, but if your eye is bad, your whole body will be full of darkness" (Mt. 6:22b–23a). "Healthy" means generous. "Bad" means "stingy." If your eyes are concentrating on granting goods to others, your entire body (or life) will be filled with light (or holiness). But if your eyes are concentrating on grasping goods for yourself, your entire body will be filled with darkness. Whatever captures your attention affects your direction.

Brother Lawrence and "Practicing the Presence"

What's needed, therefore, is a discipline designed to direct our focus. What's needed is a way to keep our attention on God and godliness rather than on goods and godlessness. "Practicing the Presence" provides this much-needed help.

The habit is rooted deeply in Scripture and in the lives of the earliest believers. But its contemporary form comes to us from two men: Brother Lawrence and Frank Laubach.[13] Brother Lawrence was born Nicolas Herman in 1611 in France. He entered the world in relative poverty. When he was fifty-five, Lawrence joined a religious community of Carmelites in Paris as a lay brother. There he took the name Brother Lawrence. His primary role in the community was that of kitchen helper. He lived the remaining years of his life tightly knit to this brotherhood, dying in 1691. We know him primarily through letters he wrote to others and through four "conversations" others wrote about him.

Lawrence became widely known in spiritual circles because of his habit of keeping God constantly on his mind: "I made it my business to be in the Lord's presence just as much throughout the day as I did when I came to my appointed time of prayer. I drove anything from my mind that was capable of interrupting my thought of God. I did this all the time, every hour, every minute, even in the height of my daily business."[14] This was the core of what came to be known as "Practicing the Presence of God"–being conscious of God all day, even in the height of daily business.

Lawrence described the custom as a "continual conversation": "You need to accustom yourself to continual conversation with Him–a conversation which is free and simple. We need to recognize that God is always intimately present with us and address Him every moment."[15] Lawrence thus urged an ongoing chat with the God who is close at all times.

This awareness of God's presence during the day grew out of Bother Lawrence's awareness of God during his dedicated times of devotion. The entire day became a kind of "quiet time": "I began to use my regular times of devotion in the same way I did the rest of my time, in fixing my mind on the presence of God... My set times for prayer are exactly like the rest of the day to me. They are but a continuation of the same exercise of being in God's presence."[16]

None of this came easily, however. Practicing the Presence required tirelessness and time. An entire decade passed before Lawrence achieved a measure of success: "This new practice revealed to me even more of the worth of the Lord... That was the beginning. The next ten years were very hard, and I suffered a great deal..."[17] The habit's simplicity belies its difficulty. But for Lawrence, and for us, the consequences are worth the cost. By changing our attention all day long, we also change our direction all day long.

Lawrence's best advice to those who sought to follow in his footsteps was this: "Forget him the very least you can."[18] The ultimate goal is to remember God the most you can. But the starting point is this: forget him the least you can.

TAKE ⑩

This discipline doesn't take ten minutes. In fact, it doesn't require any time at all. This is a habit to be practiced in the midst of everything else you do. As you eat breakfast, rush to school or work, change a diaper, fold laundry, complete a report, return e-mails, fix dinner, wash dishes, or pick up around the house, strive to focus on and be aware of and converse with God. Focus on God and his presence even in the height of your daily business. Thus, today, forget God the very least you can.

33

Making God's Presence Your Greatest Possession

God's Presence and Our Possessions

Derek Thompson, a senior editor for The Atlantic, shares how certain items have gone from luxury to necessity.[19] In 1900, less than 10 percent of families owned a stove or had access to electricity or phones. In 1915, less than 10 percent of families owned a car. In 1930, less than 10 percent of families owned a refrigerator or clothes washer. In 1945, less than 10 percent of families owned a clothes dryer or air conditioning. In 1960, less than 10 percent of families owned a dishwasher or color TV. In 1975, less than 10 percent of families owned a microwave. In 1990, less than 10 percent of families had a cell phone or access to the Internet. But today, at least 90 percent of the country has a stove, electricity, car, fridge, clothes washer, air conditioning, color TV, microwave, and cell phone. Thompson concludes, "They make our lives better. They might even make us happier. But they are not enough." Life becomes a frantic pursuit to grab for ourselves what was once only owned by the elite. Yet the grabbing never seems to end. There's always one more thing possessed by the 10 percent. And our hearts can't seem to rest until they find rest in that one more thing. Yet there is another way to live.

A growing awareness of God's presence in our daily lives affects our perspective on possessions in at least three ways.

- First, we grow in trusting that God will provide all that is needed. As we spend hour by hour in connection with him, we recognize that he cares genuinely about us and will provide generously for us. The greater our ongoing experience of God's charity, the smaller our experience of anxiety regarding possessions.

- Second, we grow in partnering with God to share all that is required. Our constant consciousness of God's presence with us gives way to a constant consciousness of his passion for those around us. We are filled not only with the enduring thought of his desire to bless us but his wish to bless others through us. Our treasures thus become a tool to make this happen.
- Third, we grow in recognizing that God is all that we've ever desired. Our constant union with him persuades us that God is a far more fulfilling pursuit than wealth or riches. His presence fills us with greater joy than any property ever could.

It may seem at first that growing in awareness of God's presence in our lives and growing in our ability to release possessions for the glory of God and the good of others are wholly unrelated. There is, however, a direct connection. As I learn that God is near and that each action of mine can honor him, this perspective eventually makes its way to my wallet. My credit cards, cash, and coins become means by which I may serve the Father and those whom he's placed around me. This is why the discipline of Practicing the Presence is so critical to moving toward a life in which we are generous with our possessions.

Laubach on Practicing the Presence

The habit that makes this nearness of God possible is called Practicing the Presence of God. In the previous chapter, we sat at the feet of Brother Lawrence as he coached us in this discipline. In this chapter we sit at the feet of a second master, Frank Laubach. Laubach was born in the United States in 1884. In the 1930s he became a Christian missionary to Muslims in the Philippines. He wrote over fifty books and was a well-known educator. He died in 1970.

Both Brother Lawrence and Frank Laubach were dedicated to a custom that became known as Practicing the Presence of God. Through this practice, both attempted to live literally each minute enjoying God's company and participating in his calling.

Laubach was especially driven by this question: "One question now to be put to the test is this: Can we have that contact with God all the time?... Or are there periods when business, and pleasures, and crowding companions must necessarily push God out of our thoughts?... Can I bring the Lord back in my mindflow every few seconds so that God shall always be in my mind?"[20] To this Laubach devoted himself. For example, he wrote in his journal on January 3, 1930: "As for me, I resolved that I would succeed better this year with my experiment of filling every minute full of the thoughts of God than I succeeded last year."[21] Later that year he indicated that he was attempting to bring God to his mind every half hour or fifteen minutes: "Two years ago a profound distraction led me to begin trying to line up my actions with the will of God about every fifteen minutes or every half hour. Other people to whom I confessed this intention said it was impossible... It is clear that this is exactly what Jesus was doing all day every year."[22] Laubach engaged God as he went about his own daily routines: "The thought of God slips out of my sight for I suppose two-thirds of every day, thus far. This morning I started out fresh, by finding a rich experience of God in the sunrise. Then I tried to let Him control my hands while I was shaving and dressing and eating breakfast. Now I am trying to let God control my hands as I pound the typewriter keys."[23]

Laubach showed that it is possible to relate with God in the routine of life. It is possible to connect meaningfully to God in the common moments of life. This, in turn, transforms the ordinary into the extraordinary.

Recommendations for Practicing the Presence

How do we start? How do we move into this habit? Here are ten recommendations (the first seven come from Laubach, the final three come from author Adele Calhoun):[24]

1. Select a favorable hour, an easy, uncomplicated hour. See how many minutes of the hour you can remember, or touch, Christ at least once a minute; that is to say, bring Him to mind at least one second out of every sixty.

2. Keep humming to yourself (inaudibly) a favorite hymn; For example, *Have Thine Own Way, Lord, Have Thine Own Way.* You might especially hum this tune as you touch various possessions of yours through the day. As you put your dishes in the dishwasher, as you place your clothes in the drawer, as your drive your car, as you pull out your wallet to pay for lunch, hum this tune as a reminder that you want God's way with your resources.

3. When reading, keep a running conversation with Him about the pages you are reading.

4. [When considering some problem] "Instead of talking to yourself, form the habit of talking to Christ. This may be especially rewarding while you are out shopping. Talk to Christ about these purchases. If you are grocery shopping, give thanks to Christ for the abundance he's provided–the tasty green beans, the juicy meat, the sweet ice cream, etc.

5. Make sure that your last thoughts are of Christ as you are falling asleep at night.

6. On waking in the morning, you may ask, "Now, Lord, shall we get up?" Some of us whisper to Him in our every thought about washing and dressing in the morning.

7. We need the stimulus of believers who pursue what we pursue, the presence of Christ. (That is, find some others who are also attempting to practice the presence and spur on one another.)

8. With each task during the day, talk to God about the task before you begin and when you are finished. It will be especially helpful to do this when you are engaged in any financial task. Whether making deposits or withdrawals at the bank, paying bills online, or writing out a shopping list, speak to God as you do these things.

9. Set an alarm for several times throughout the day. At each alarm stop and pray. Consider choosing a verse that focuses on possessions.

10. Memorize a short verse or short prayer and repeat it throughout the day.

TAKE ⑩

As I mentioned in the previous chapter, this habit doesn't take ten minutes. We practice this discipline while doing everything else that makes up our day. So today, try one of the ten tips above. Enjoy God's company and participate in his calling in everything you do today.

34

Finding God in Your Backyard

Practicing the Presence grows from the soil of two certainties about God. Both Testaments testify to this pair of divine realities. In the New Testament, Paul builds on these realities as he introduces non-Christians to the Christian faith:

So Paul, standing in the midst of the Areopagus, said: "Men of Athens, I perceive that in every way you are very religious. For as I passed along and observed the objects of your worship, I found also an altar with this inscription, 'To the unknown god.' What therefore you worship as unknown, this I proclaim to you. The God who made the world and everything in it, being Lord of heaven and earth, does not live in temples made by man, nor is he served by human hands, as though he needed anything, since he himself gives to all mankind life and breath and everything. And he made from one man every nation of mankind to live on all the face of the earth, having determined allotted periods and the boundaries of their dwelling place, that they should seek God, and perhaps feel their way toward him and find him. Yet he is actually not far from each one of us, for

'In him we live and move and have our being';
  as even some of your own poets have said,
'For we are indeed his offspring.'

Being then God's offspring, we ought not to think that the divine being is like gold or silver or stone, an image formed by the art and imagination of man. The times of ignorance God overlooked, but now he commands all people everywhere to repent, because he has fixed a day on which he will judge the world in righteousness by a man whom he has appointed; and of this he has given assurance to all by raising him from the dead." (Acts 17:22–31)

In this sermon, Paul critiques the way the Athenians viewed God. They would never appreciate who Jesus was if they didn't first apprehend who God was. New Testament scholar D. A. Carson notes some of the ways in which Paul confronts their incorrect views of God's identity:[25]

1. Contrary to the ancient pagan assumption that gods rule only over a particular domain (e.g., Neptune and the sea), Paul states that the true God is "Lord of heaven and earth" and "does not live in temples made by man" (Acts 17:24). God is king of all domains.
2. In opposition to the polytheistic notion of gods whose needs must be met by humans, Paul proclaims that the true God "is [not] served by human hands, as though he needed anything" (17:25). God is self-existent and entirely independent from us. Though we need him desperately, he does not need us.
3. Despite God's autonomy from us, Paul then reveals God's affection for us. Paul does not want to leave any impression that his is a deistic God. Thus he affirms that God "is not far from each one of us" (17:27). God is not just independent (and thus distant). He is also imminent (and thus nearby). God stays close to us, for he longs to be connected with us.

Paul's audience was living by a narrative in which two things were true about the gods: the gods were domestic and deistic. Ancient pagan religions held that the gods are domestic—they dwell in one particular geographical region, political nation, or religious temple. If you wanted to converse with or connect to a certain god, you had to be in his or her "neighborhood." Only after you crossed the correct geographical, political, or religious boundary was that god accessible.

In addition, ancient religions regarded the gods as deistic—they made the cosmos and the creatures, set the whole machine in motion, and now watch from a distance. They may hold the world in their hands, but they are definitely not close at hand.

Paul discloses that the Christian God is different. Our God is not domestic. He is not constrained by geography, limited by politics, or localized to a temple. He is the "Lord of heaven and earth." God's quarters are the cosmos. He is accessible from any topography, nationality, or sanctuary. He may be discovered as easily from a park bench or a preschool as from the mountaintop or the Holy Land.

Paul also shows that our God is not deistic. He is not watching from a distance. He is working in our midst. He seeks not seclusion from us but affiliation with us. He wishes not that we would leave him alone but that he would never leave us alone. He has not finished his work of creation and handed it over to us. He's continuing his work of recreation and hoping to do it with us and through us.

Everywhere Engaged

In other words, God is not domestic–he is everywhere. And God is not deistic–he is engaged.

God is everywhere. He may be found wherever we find ourselves: at the sink brushing our teeth, in the nursery changing a diaper, in a cubicle completing a report, or on an airplane 30,000 feet above the ground.

And God is engaged. He is not isolated from the daily grind; he's not removed from the routine and regular. God is not retired; he is employed from sunrise to sundown. He is engrossed from dusk to dawn. His hands are dirty and calloused from his ongoing labor of love. Wherever you step, you can trust that God's already at work.

In short, God is everywhere engaged.

Paul the letter writer isn't the only one to highlight these divine qualities. David the poem writer does as well. Notice Psalm 139. This stirring sonnet is a protest of sorts. David uses poetry to show that God is not deistic but near and intimately involved in human life.

O Lord, you have searched me and known me!
You know when I sit down and when I rise up;
  you discern my thoughts from afar.
You search out my path and my lying down
  and are acquainted with all my ways.
Even before a word is on my tongue,
  behold, O Lord, you know it altogether.
You hem me in, behind and before,
  and lay your hand upon me.
Such knowledge is too wonderful for me;
  it is high; I cannot attain it…
For you formed my inward parts;
  you knitted me together in my mother's womb.
I praise you, for I am fearfully and wonderfully made.
Wonderful are your works;
  my soul knows it very well.
My frame was not hidden from you,
when I was being made in secret,
  intricately woven in the depths of the earth.
Your eyes saw my unformed substance;

in your book were written, every one of them,
  the days that were formed for me,
  when as yet there was none of them.
How precious to me are your thoughts, O God!
  How vast is the sum of them!
If I would count them, they are more than the sand.
I awake, and I am still with you. (Ps. 139:1–6, 13–18)

God knows the thoughts in David's mind. He knows words about to be on David's lips. Through both the rearview mirror and windshield David sees God. God is behind him and before him. Everywhere David is, God is. Everywhere David will be, God is. From David's mother's womb to his sheep's pasture to his nation's throne, God knows (and wrote) the whole book on David. This God is engaged in every page of David's novel.

David also uses verses to illustrate that God is not domestic but lives and dwells everywhere a person might imagine going:

Where shall I go from your Spirit?
  Or where shall I flee from your presence?
If I ascend to heaven, you are there!
  If I make my bed in Sheol, you are there!
If I take the wings of the morning
  and dwell in the uttermost parts of the sea,
even there your hand shall lead me,
  and your right hand shall hold me.
If I say, "Surely the darkness shall cover me,
  and the light about me be night,"
even the darkness is not dark to you;
  the night is bright as the day,
  for darkness is as light with you. (Ps. 139:7–12)

God can be encountered high in the heavens and low in the grave. At the completion of the longest flight we might undertake, we'll find God already waiting for us at the arrival gate. Even at the bottom of the darkest and deepest valley of the shadow of death, we find the Father waiting. This God is everywhere. He is everywhere engaged.

Practicing the Presence

Practicing the Presence is an attempt to fully embrace the fact that God is everywhere engaged. Every scene of your life today–from bedroom to boardroom to backyard–has been a place where God was present and interested in partnering with you. God is accessible at any moment on the clock and any location on the map. There is more of God available to you in this present moment and in your current situation than you can possibly imagine. If you lived your remaining years stuck in the next sixty seconds or caught where you currently sit or stand, you could not exhaust all God wishes to give you of himself. He is everywhere, and everywhere he seeks to engage us. Practicing the Presence of God is an attempt to stay consciously aware of him as much as possible throughout the day and to interact with him throughout the day.

Richard Foster calls this practice "unceasing prayer" and writes that it is "the best, the finest, the fullest way of living."[26] What makes this such a fine way of living? Mark Buchanan tells us:

> When we practice the presence of God, we train ourselves to desire His presence—to resist our temptation to flee Him. We also train ourselves to experience His presence—to resist our temptation to think that he flees us. In other words, the practice of the presence of God helps us to live between the temptations of Jonah bound for Tarshish and John bound in prison. Jonah is the prophet who wants to abandon God. John is the prophet who feels abandoned by God. When we practice the presence of God, we refuse to live in either sense of abandonment.[27]

Make this habit an ongoing part of your life and you'll never again wish to flee the Father for something far less fulfilling. And you'll never again fear that the Father has fled you because of your latest failing.

TAKE ⑩

Take a few minutes right now to consider this question: If God is everywhere I go today and is deeply engaged in my life in all those places, how would this affect my behavior? Now go and live in that light.

35

Taking the Remedy of Simplicity

In his book *Things Unseen*, Mark Buchanan talks about our constant craving:

> I saw this close-up…when my children first got to that age when the essence of Christmas becomes The Day of Getting. There were mounds of gifts beneath our tree, and our son led the way in that favorite childhood (and, more subtly, adult) game, How Many Are for Me? But the telling moment came Christmas morning when the gifts were handed out. The children ripped through them, shredding and scattering the wrappings like jungle plants before a well-wielded machete… When the ransacking was finished, my son, standing amid a tumultuous sea of boxes and bright crumpled paper and exotic trappings, asked plaintively, "Is this all there is?"[28]

This craving, which may appear harmless, is actually hazardous. Paul reveals the danger of such desires in a trio of letters called the "pastoral" letters. These letters are addressed to "pastors" named Timothy and Titus whom Paul had commissioned over a few specific congregations.[29] A survey of the correspondence shows that these churches were perishing from spiritual poisons. This becomes clear through Paul's frequent use of the word sound. The word means "healthy." The "patient charts" for these congregations show that Paul is deeply concerned about their soundness. For example, he writes about people who are teaching things "contrary to sound doctrine" (1 Tim. 1:10). He urges Timothy to follow the "sound words" that Paul taught him (2 Tim. 1:13). Paul petitions elders to be able to teach "sound doctrine" and to refute those who contradict it (Titus 1:9, emphasis added in the previous scripture quotes). What most concerns Paul about these saints is the question of their soundness. We can surmise that he writes so often about health because this is the very quality most in danger among them.

As a good physician, Paul diagnoses the sources of their sickness. Some of the symptoms are the result of common causes. For example, Paul warns of those who are "lovers of self," "abusive," "unholy," "heartless," "brutal," "swollen with conceit," and "lovers of pleasure rather than lovers of God" (2 Tim. 3:2–4). You don't need an M.D. to understand how heartlessness or hedonism could lead to spiritual disease in a Christian community. But Paul also points to a cause rarely acknowledged by even the best Christian medics. He identifies something as "harmful," which many view as harmless:

- "Therefore an overseer must not [be] a lover of *money* (1 Tim. 3:2–3)
- "Deacons likewise must not [be] greedy for dishonest *gain* (1 Tim. 3:8)
- "For the love of *money* is a root of all kinds of evils (1 Tim. 6:10a)
- "But understand this, that in the last days there will come times of difficulty. For people will be lovers of self, lovers of *money* (2 Tim. 3:1–2a)
- "For an overseer must not be *greedy* for gain (Titus 1:7)

Paul believes the wealth of the church is one of the largest threats to the church's health. He thinks that finances greatly impact fitness. Some of the greatest spiritual diseases in our lives will stem from the misuse of money, the craving for cash, the desire for dough.

Jesus points to this same malady in his Sermon on the Mount. He warns listeners not to "lay up for yourselves treasures on earth" (Mt. 6:19). He states that it is impossible to serve God while also serving money (v. 24). He cautions against our obsession with commodities such as clothing and chow (v. 6:25–34).

We can have correct creeds. We may perform worship wonderfully. Our rituals may be the best of any religion. Yet even with these we can be unsound. Even with these we can be unwell. The wealth of the church too often is one of the largest threats to the health of the church.

Common Cures for Craving

Richard Foster finds that Christians have applied three cures to this disease. Each, he proposes, comes in the form of a vow.[30] First, some have responded with a vow of poverty. They have attempted to do what the rich man who came to Jesus could not do—sell all possessions for the sake of the poor. Jesus may ask some to do this. There may be some of us who need to renounce our resources. But not all in Scripture were called to the vow of poverty. Many godly people in Scripture did not surrender their goods and give all to those in need.

Second, some Christians have responded with a vow of industry. If the vow of poverty is most closely associated with the monks, the vow of industry is tied to the Puritans. Being industrious became synonymous with being godly. A saint was one who labored hard and reaped the fruit of his labor. Unfortunately, the vow of industry ultimately led to less than godly attitudes. The more industrious and hard-working one became, the more wealth one earned, and the more wealth one wanted.

Foster suggests that Scripture points toward a third vow that Christians can and should take. It is a vow that enables us to possess without misusing and mistrusting possessions. It is a vow that ensures God's will is done with the goods over which he's made us stewards. It is a vow that avoids the problems of the vow of poverty and the vow of industry. He calls it the vow of simplicity. Simplicity is the solution to our lack of soundness. Simplicity is the cure for our consumerism and craving.

The Practice of Simplicity

This is probably something for which you already long. Father and son Thom and Art Rainer once asked more than one thousand Americans about their pace of life.[31] They found that a vast majority of us are longing for simpler lives. We want more balance and less busyness. We desire increased flexibility and decreased complexity. We yearn for time to just enjoy life. Specifically, the Rainers found that we seek simplicity in four areas:

- Schedules: we want a better balance in our schedules so that we have time for areas of life that really matter to us.
- Relationships: we long for better and closer relationships and friendships.
- Finances: we dream of lives free from past-due bills, diminishing income, or increasing debt.
- Spirituality: we are too busy for God and need a simpler life in order to grow closer to him.

The authors write:

Busyness has consumed us. In our survey we were amazed to see that approximately 44 percent of respondents agreed that if their daily life continued at the current pace, they would probably have health problems... Of course, not just our physical health is suffering. Our families are also impacted... Some 57 percent of married survey respondents admitted that they rarely are able to go on a date with their spouses... We asked if their family members were able to relax and enjoy one another. Only 13 percent agreed strongly that they could... In our survey more than 45 percent of the respondents admitted that they did not have enough income for their lifestyles. For many of us, money is a ball and chain attached around the ankle, limiting our life's movement. Nearly seven out of ten...said that they needed to spend more time on spiritual matters.[32]

A more simple life is a key toward living into Jesus' vision for our lives. This is particularly true regarding his vision for our possessions. Like Practicing the Presence, simplicity is a discipline that does not require much time at all. It is a position we take in our minds as much as it is a practice we engage in with our hands. Simplicity is one of the most powerful medicines against the ailment of greed and consumerism.

TAKE ⑩

Here are some simple suggestions for streamlining your life.[33] Read through them. Choose one to focus on and practice today.

1. If you haven't used a possession in a year or more, get rid of it.
2. Move to a smaller house.
3. Drive a simple car.
4. Sell the boat.
5. Build a simple wardrobe.
6. Reduce your entertainment expenses.
7. Simplify meals when you have others over.
8. Turn off the television.
9. Cancel most magazine subscriptions.
10. Don't answer the phone just because it's ringing.
11. Simplify gift giving.
12. Take a vacation at home.
13. Live on half of what you earn.
14. Allow purchases on only one day per week.
15. Delay major purchases for two weeks.

16. Get rid of all but one or two credit cards.
17. Work where you live, or live where you work.
18. Always split a restaurant meal.
19. Make water your drink of choice.
20. Pack your lunch.
21. Drive the speed limit.
22. If it's not working, stop doing it.

36

Giving Up the Good Life

The Good Life vs. the Abundant Life

Speaker and writer Michael Schut explains that most of us are missing the "abundant life" because we are caught up with the "good life."[34] The good life is the American dream. Two-story house. Two-car garage. Two children. Two pets. Two incomes. The lake house. The gym. The golf clubs and cruises. It's the lifestyle promoted by TV, billboards, newspapers, magazines, and cultural leaders. This way of living is based on the equation funds + finances = fun and fulfillment. Productivity and activity are applauded. The good life values self and human desires above all else. In reality, though, the good life winds down like an old toy and must be constantly rewound. Moreover, the so-called good life leads to busyness, fatigue, and increasing chaos.

Psychologist James Dobson tells a story about the gut-wrenching impact of the good life:

> Several months ago, I talked to a man who described one of the most painful experiences of his life. When he was 17 years old, he was one of the stars on his high school football team. But his father, a very successful man in the city, was always too busy to come see him play. The final game of the season came around, which happened to have been the state championship. The boy was desperate to have his dad there. The night of the big game, he was on the field, warming up, when he looked into the stadium just in time to see his father arrive with two other men, each wearing a business suit. They stood talking together for a moment or two and then left. The man who told me this story is now 58 years of age, and yet

he had tears streaming down his cheeks as he relived that moment so long ago. It's been 40 years since that night, and yet the rejection and pain are as vivid as ever. I was struck again by the awesome influence a father has in the lives of his children. My friend's father died not long ago, and as he stood by his dad's body in the mortuary, he said: "Dad, I never really knew you. We could have shared so much love together–but you never had time for me."[35]

Much of the chaos and clutter of our lives is caused by the fact that we've chosen to focus on satisfying our needs as the good life defines them. But a life spent in the pursuit of success and savings leads only to shattered lives and staggering loss.

Life doesn't have to be lived this way. There is an alternative, and it's called the "abundant life." This life is not the American dream. It's the Almighty's dream. The abundant life is about having a little and loving a lot. This way of life involves rich relationships and lavish love. It leads to freedom–the freedom to define self in terms of relationship with God rather than with goods. Freedom to live a theology of enough, which reminds us that we may already have more than we need so we don't need any more. The abundant life is deep, vibrant, and constant.

C. S. Lewis writes about these two ways of living and how they differ:

> The Biological sort which comes to us through Nature, and which (like everything else in Nature) is always tending to run down and decay so that it can only be kept up by incessant subsidies from Nature in the form of air, water, food, etc. is Bios. The Spiritual life which is in God from all eternity, and which made the whole universe, is Zoe. Bios has, to be sure, a certain shadowy or symbolic resemblance to Zoe: but only the sort of resemblance there is between a photo and a place, or a statue and a man.[36]

Bios is the natural life, which winds down and decays. Zoe is the spiritual life, which persists and remains vibrant. What many of us seek is bios–the good life. What all of us need is zoe–the abundant life.

Gaining Through Contentment

But how do we exchange the good life for the abundant life? One way is through the practice of simplicity, for simplicity stems from an attitude of contentment. Donald Whitney writes, "No one will satisfyingly simplify his spiritual life without contentment."[37] And contentment, Whitney suggests, comes through two things: learning the true value of things and learning the true value of Christ. One of the greatest hindrances to our happiness is that we overvalue stuff and we undervalue the Savior, we overrate resources and underrate relationships. But once we grasp the true value of Christ and his Way, we find contentment and are no longer distracted with the pursuit of the good life. Life becomes simpler and more satisfying.

Richard Foster writes that contentment comes from three perspectives.[38] First, we learn to view possessions as gifts from God. All our material goods are gifts from above. Second, we view these gifts as things to be cared for by God. God is able to protect what he's granted to us. We can trust him and thus need not worry over these resources. Finally, we understand these things given to us by God and cared for by God are to be made available to others. We do all we can to supply the needs of others through what God has given to us. These three perspectives lead to contentment and thus to simplicity.

The opposite three attitudes lead to fretfulness and stress. If we view things in our possession purely as the fruits of our own labor, and something we alone must protect, and if we do not make them available for others, eventually we are led into anxiety and worry. Contentment and simplicity become impossible.

TAKE ⑩

Simplicity is a process. We take small steps in its direction. Here are some more simple suggestions by which you can do just that.[39] Choose one to focus on and practice today.

23. Stop trying to change people.
24. Don't multitask.
25. Say "No."
26. Resign from any organizations whose meetings you dread.
27. Welcome delays as an opportunity to relax.
28. Do nothing from time to time.
29. Ask others for help.
30. Take time for lunch.
31. Finish this statement: If my life were simplified, I would feel...
32. Complete this sentence: To me a simple life means...
33. Consider this matter: What keeps me from simplifying my life is...
34. Finish this practical hypothetical: If I were to simplify my life, I would...

35. Stress the quality of your life above the quantity of your life.
36. Make recreation healthy, happy, and gadget-free.
37. Eat out less.
38. When you do eat out, make it a celebration.
39. Become as acquainted with people as with places.
40. Buy things for their usefulness rather than their status.
41. Buy only what you need.
42. Wear your clothes until they are worn out.
43. Impress people with your life, not your clothes.
44. Give generously.

37

Uncluttering Your Heart

Traveling Light

In the book All Is Calm, minister Donna Schaper tells of the harsh reality of trying to take too much on the journey:

> There we were, two people in love, on the rim of the Grand Canyon on New Year's Eve, watching the sun go down and realizing that the hotel really was full... My husband had a brainstorm. "I'll bet the ranger in the bottom of the canyon is lonely, especially tonight. Let's call him and see how he would feel about some guests." The idea had merit: Its desperation matched our own. The telephone number of the canyon ranger was right in the book. We dialed, explained our situation, and offered a barter of groceries packed down. Gary, the ranger, said that he and his most-pregnant wife would love company and would especially enjoy company that brought guacamole and tortilla chips. The hardest part of the evening was finding avocados at 6 p.m. We did find them, and didn't mind paying the astronomical price. A half-hour after dusk, we were on our way down... Gina, Gary's wife, had come on the phone and insisted that we "bring nothing" but the chips and dip. She kept saying, "We have everything." Little did we know. We arrived near midnight, after a light but uneventful passage down the curving canyon.... We knocked on the door and were surprised to be greeted by an ordinary couple about our age. Gina looked eight, maybe 12 months pregnant. They were dressed casually. They let

us into their large cabin and served us a nice dinner... They showed us their "sports room." It was full of abandoned sports equipment. High-class hiking boots. High-class backpacks. Fancy hats, fancier walking sticks. Three-hundred-dollar down vests. "People can walk in easily enough with all this stuff; they just can't walk out," Gina told us.[40]

Would you stop for a minute and take inventory of all that's in your life's pack today? The tasks. The worries. The regrets. The appointments. The obligations. The e-mails. The voicemails. The errands. The projects. It's probably more than you realized, isn't it? When each new item comes along, we tend to think, "I can walk in with that." But it all begins to weigh us down. And in the end we can't walk out. How do we lighten our load? How do we unpack and repack? Most of us want to travel light. We just don't know how.

Inward Simplicity

No one packed as light as Jesus. He had no house of his own. His possessions were the clothing on his back and sandals on his feet. Of course, he had no smart phone pinging with e-mails and appointments. Jesus lived a modest and uncluttered life.

My friend Gary Holloway points out that this outward simplicity was made possible by Jesus' inward simplicity.[41] His heart was uncluttered. Only one call commanded his heart's attention. Only one task demanded his energy. Because of this, he was able to speak the one word that makes simplicity possible: "No." Jesus did not heal every patient. He did not teach every person. He did not travel to every place. He said "No" to many items and individuals so he could say "Yes" to a few. His well-ordered life flowed from a well-ordered heart.

Jesus invites us to possess this same heart when he says in his Sermon on the Mount, "But seek first the kingdom of God and his righteousness, and all these things will be added to you" (Mt. 6:33). Once the heart's drive is devoted primarily to "seeking first" God's dominion, decisions become clearer and life becomes simpler. In fact, we can view the entire Sermon on the Mount as Jesus' attempt to make us "pure in heart" (Mt. 5:8). When your heart is unpolluted by the toxins of hundreds of human "have-to's" and is clarified by one divine "must-do," simplicity becomes possible.

What is God's "must-do" in your life? That's the most important question to answer in order to take a step toward untangling and uncomplicating your life.

Giving Up the Exceptional Life

One thing muddying up life for many of us is our pursuit of what Richard Foster calls the "exceptional life." In his book Freedom of Simplicity, Foster observes that many of us try to live beyond our financial and emotional means.[42] Financially, we spend too much, want too much, and waste too much. Emotionally, we work too hard, rest too little, and fill our schedule too full. The result is drained souls and savings.

Why do we do this? It stems from our desire to have the exceptional life. We want to have it all. We desire the highest level in our career, an ideal family life, exciting recreation and hobbies, notoriety and fame. But in striving for everything, we can wind up with nothing. Pursuing the exceptional life comes at a high cost. We cannot live beyond our means for long without getting burned out, stressed out, and used up.

Simplicity arrives when this internal hunger is replaced with another. As we abandon the pursuit of the exceptional life and nurture a passion for the Jesus-life, we experience a change of heart. This translates into a change of pace. And living beyond our means becomes a thing of the past.

TAKE ⑩

Sometimes a small external change can help spark an internal change. Here are some additional simple suggestions.[43] Pick one to focus on and practice today:

45. Serve sacrificially.
46. Learn to enjoy things without owning them.
47. Receive what you have as a gift, not an entitlement.
48. Reject anything that is producing an addiction in you.
49. Develop a habit of giving things away.
50. Look with healthy skepticism on all "buy now, pay later" schemes.
51. Reject anything that breeds the oppression of others.
52. Shun anything that distracts you from seeking first the kingdom of God.
53. Ruthlessly eliminate hurry.
54. Deliberately drive in the slow lane.
55. Declare a fast from honking.
56. For a week, eat your food slowly.
57. Get in the longest check-out line.
58. Go one day without wearing a watch.

59. If you haven't worn it in a year, get rid of it.
60. If you have to do complicated logarithms to justify something, don't buy it.
61. Resolve relationship conflict.
62. Spend some time in solitude.
63. Focus just on loving God and loving people.
64. Keep the main thing the main thing.
65. Don't schedule or attend meetings back to back.
66. Make a budget.

38

Putting Happiness
Back into Holiness

A man once approached me at the gym where I exercise. We live in the same neighborhood, work out in the same weight room, and have had several conversations about our Christian faith. That morning he asked an odd question: "When someone gets baptized at your church, do people clap?" This issue had come up at his church recently. Someone had clapped at a baptism as a gesture of joy and my friend and others were uncomfortable with it. He said, "We clap at ballgames, not at baptisms." My rec center companion was saying that it's proper to party when a grown man hits a ball with a stick, but it's wrong to revel when a person is washed by the Son, filled with the Spirit, and embraced by the Father. Had I pressed him on this, I think he would have backpedaled.

Why do Christians have such a problem with pleasure? For some, the challenge is theological. We hold to a doctrine so packed with reverence and remorse that there's no room for elation and exultation. We're so persuaded that we ought to be somber and serious that we can't imagine being gleeful and glad. For others, the challenge is circumstantial. There always seems to be something wrong. Work is too hectic, school is too hard, or the weather is too hot. There seems to be nothing worth smiling about from sunrise to sunset. For far too many of us, joy is not a defining trait of our Christian faith.

A few years ago Christian author Brennan Manning proposed that joy is the great divider in the United States:

> I believe that the real difference in the American church is
> not between conservatives and liberals, fundamentalists and

charismatics, nor between Republicans and Democrats. The real difference is between the aware and the unaware. When somebody is aware of that love–the same love that the Father has for Jesus–that person is just spontaneously grateful. Cries of thankfulness become the dominant characteristic of the interior life, and the byproduct of gratitude is joy.[44]

In other words, the real separation among American Christians is between those who live with joy and those who do not.

This struggle with enjoyment not only affects the quality of our lives. It radically impacts the way we approach our possessions. The greater our delight in what we already have in life, the less hunger we have for those things we do not have. But the less our joy for what we presently possess, the greater our desire for more. Joy is what makes the difference between a person filled with contentment and a person driven by craving. It's tricky to be overwhelmingly generous with our possessions when we are underwhelmingly filled with joy.

Philippians, Prison, and Joy

That's why it is so helpful to spend time with Paul and his letter to the Philippians. Paul is stuck in a situation where joy seems impossible. He is in jail. And this wasn't the only time he was in chains. He spent roughly one-quarter of his missionary career behind bars. These ancient jails were places that obliterated joy:

Roman imprisonment was preceded by being stripped naked and then flogged–a humiliating, painful, and bloody ordeal. The bleeding wounds went untreated as prisoners sat in painful leg or wrist chains. Mutilated, bloodstained clothing was not replaced, even in the cold of winter. Most cells were dark, especially the inner cells of a prison, like the one Paul and Silas inhabited in Philippi. Unbearable cold, lack of water, cramped quarters, and sickening stench from few toilets made sleeping difficult and waking hours miserable. Because of the miserable conditions, many prisoners begged for a speedy death. Others simply committed suicide.[45]

Paul writes his letter to the Philippians from a spot where others are so sad they are contemplating suicide.

Yet the word used again and again in Paul's letter is the word *joy,* or *rejoice:*

- "In all my prayers for all of you, I always pray with *joy*." (Phil. 1:4, NIV)
- "But what does it matter? The important thing is that in every way, whether from false motives or true, Christ is preached.

And because of this I *rejoice*. Yes, and I will continue to *rejoice*."
(1:18, NIV)

- "Convinced of this, I know that I will remain, and I will
  continue with all of you for your progress and *joy* in the faith,"
  (1:25, NIV)
- "... then make my *joy* complete by being like-minded, having
  the same love, being one in spirit and of one mind." (2:2, NIV)
- "But even if I am being poured out like a drink offe*ring* on
  t*he sacr*ifice and service coming from your faith, I am *glad* and
  rejoice with all of you." (2:17, NIV)
- "So you too should be *glad* and *rejoice* with me." (2:18, NIV)
- "Welcome him in the Lord with great *joy,* and honor people
  like him." (2:29, NIV)
- "Further, my brothers and sisters, *rejoice* in the Lord! It is no
  trouble for me to write the same things to you again, and it is a
  safeguard for you." (3:1, NIV)
- "Therefore, my brothers *and* sisters, you whom I love and long
  for, my *joy* and crown, stand firm in the Lord in this way, dear
  friends!" (4:1, NIV)
- "*Rejoice* in the Lord always. I will say it again: *Rejoice!*" (4:4,
  NIV)
- "I *rejoiced* greatly in the Lord that at last you have renewed
  your concern for me." (4:10, NIV) (*Emphasis added in all quotes
  above.*)

In spite of unbearable circumstances, joy was still a defining
characteristic of Paul's Christian faith. In fact, Paul writes this: "I have
learned the secret of being content in any and every situation, whether
well fed or hungry, whether living in plenty or in want" (Phil. 4:12b,
NIV). The word translated "secret" was used in pagan religions to
refer to mysteries of life that only those who practiced that religion
could unravel.[46] Pagan religions had secrets and privileges that were
reserved only for their adherents. Paul borrows that idea to write that
the Christian faith also has a secret and a privilege for its adherents.
And that secret is contentment in any situation. In a word, joy. The
Christian faith, and only the Christian faith, discloses the secret to
experiencing a joy that is greater than expected even when conditions
are worse than anticipated.

The word *content* means to have sufficient resources, to need no
aid. It means to be self-sufficient.[47] Paul has learned the mystery of
having sufficient resources for joy regardless of the circumstances.
In spite of what he doesn't have, as long as he does have Jesus, Paul

has all he needs to experience delight. Jesus provides inexhaustible resources for indefinite joy. Nothing else is required.

Celebration

How do we move toward this happy vision of life? The wisest sages of Christianity summon us to practice the discipline of celebration. Celebration consists of tiny steps we take to express or experience joy. As we engage in these petite parties, joy begins to leak into other areas of our life until delight and contentment take over.

In his aptly named book *Celebration of Discipline*, Richard Foster offers these recommendations for growing in your ability to revel:[48]

1. Sing, dance, shout, and play like children. Get down on the ground and play, dance, and laugh in the same way your children or grandchildren do.
2. Laugh. Learn to laugh at a good joke. Learn to laugh at yourself. Make a habit of watching good comedies.
3. Take joy in the creative works of others. Listen to music. Visit a museum. Walk through some antique stores. Allow yourself to enjoy the creativity you see or hear.
4. Make family events such as birthdays, graduations, marriages, and anniversaries occasions of great joy. One of the easiest ways to move toward joy is to learn to throw and enjoy a great party. When that next special occasion comes up, make it a grand celebration.
5. Celebrate lesser events, such as finishing a project or receiving a raise. Almost every week we experience some lesser but still important victory. Learn to celebrate those.

TAKE ⑩

Take ten minutes today to put into practice one of the recommendations listed above.

39

Practicing Joy Like Jesus

Delight Disparity

In moments of honesty, when I compare myself with Jesus, I observe a "delight disparity." On the one hand, there's Jesus. He's delighted. Smiling. Laughing. Taking pleasure in people and places. On the other hand, there's me. I'm detached. Unimpressed. Dispassionate. Sometimes finding flaws in people and places. The gaiety that Jesus is so quick to express I am often quick to repress.

Perhaps I'm not the only one guilty of this offense. Richard Foster proposes that multitudes share the blame: "Jesus rejoiced so fully in life that he was accused of being a winebibber and a glutton. Many of us lead such sour lives that we cannot possibly be accused of such things."[49] There's a glaring gap between the vibrant revelry of Jesus and the monotony or misery of his followers. The sour frowns on our faces stand in such stark contrast to the satisfied grin on his.

What's the root of this disparity? For some of us it stems from our view of God. We're not sure God wants us happy. John Acuff tells of the time when his latest book, *Quitter*, was released for publication. He was in high spirits. But Acuff began to have doubts about whether God wanted him to experience pleasure through this publishing triumph:

> And in my quiet time, as I prayed that morning, this is what went through my head, "Maybe *Quitter* will fail so that God can teach you an important lesson." In the space before I had the chance to have another thought, I felt like God rushed in. It wasn't audible, it wasn't written on the wall. A bush did not catch ablaze, but in my heart this is what I felt: Why can't I teach you in the midst of joy? In what better

way could I reveal the heart of who I am, goodness, then in
the midst of something good? You believe I can only teach
you in the midst of great hardship and hurt. But failure is
not my only laboratory. Does not a father learn something
profound about my miraculous goodness when he holds his
newborn baby for the first time after delivery? Does not a
bride see my glory when she walks down the aisle toward
her groom? Life and lessons cannot be limited to heartache.
This is what I am wrestling with right now… I know how
to cry with him, but not laugh. I know how to mourn with
him but not dance.[50]

How about you? Are you skilled in mourning with God, but
sloppy in dancing with him? Do you sometimes wonder if hilarity is
contrary to spirituality?

Celebration Celebrity

If so, consider the drama of Jesus produced by Luke. In his
carefully constructed screenplay about Jesus, Luke does not cast joy
as an extra who appears in the background of a couple of shots. He
presents joy as a star who steals scene after scene.

Joy stands at the center of the first act. In chapter 1, the angel
who is speaking to Zechariah about his child says, "And you will have
joy and gladness, and many will rejoice at his birth" (Lk. 1:14). Joy
is also centerstage in the final act. In chapter 24, Luke describes the
impact of the risen and ascending Jesus: "And they worshiped him
and returned to Jerusalem with great joy" (Lk. 24:52). Luke's chronicle
of Jesus' life begins and ends with great joy.

In between these bookends, joy continues to make numerous
appearances:

- [Elizabeth says to Mary] "For behold, when the sound of your
  greeting came to my ears, the baby in my womb leaped for
  joy." (Lk. 1:44)
- [Mary sings] " and my spirit rejoices in God my Savior" (1:47)
- [Regarding Elizabeth] "And her neighbors and relatives heard
  that the Lord had shown great mercy to her, and they rejoiced
  with her." (1:58)
- [Regarding Jesus] "In that same hour he rejoiced in the Holy
  Spirit and said " (10:21a)
- [In the parable of the lost sheep, coin, and son] "And when he
  comes home, he calls together his friends and his neighbors,

saying to them, 'Rejoice with me, for I have found my sheep that was lost.'" (15:6)

- "Just so, I tell you, there will be more joy in heaven over one sinner who repents than over ninety-nine righteous persons who need no repentance." (15:7)
- "And when she has found it, she calls together her friends and neighbors, saying, 'Rejoice with me, for I have found the coin that I had lost.'" (15:9)
- [Regarding Jesus] "As he was drawing near already on the way down the Mount of Olives the whole multitude of his disciples began to rejoice and praise God with a loud voice for all the mighty works that they had seen." (19:37)

If Jesus is the star of Luke's composition, joy is the co-star. When Jesus makes an entrance, joy is often by his side.

What was true then is true now. If Jesus has entered our life, joy wants to be by his side. Author Dennis Prager once asked a deeply religious man if he considered himself a truly pious person. man said he did not. He said that he didn't think he was joyful enough to be considered truly pious. A truly pious person, the man remarked, will be full of joy. He went on to suggest that his lack of joy and the lack of joy of many Christians is a threat to the Christian faith. In response, Prager wrote these words:

> He was right; in fact, unhappy religious people pose a real challenge to faith. If their faith is so impressive, why aren't these devoted adherents happy? There are only two possible reasons: either they are not practicing their faith correctly, or they are practicing their faith correctly and the religion itself is not conducive to happiness. Most outsiders assume the latter reason. Unhappy religious people should therefore think about how important being happy is—if not for themselves, then for the sake of their religion. Unhappy, let alone angry, religious people provide more persuasive arguments for atheism and secularism than do all the arguments of atheists.[51]

Joy is the ultimate apologetic—convincing proof to a watching world that life with Jesus is immeasurably better than life without him. That's why it is so important to reduce, as much as possible, any delight disparity which has made a home in our hearts.

Celebration

The habit of celebration shows the way to overcome the delight disparity. In one sense, celebration is part of every spiritual discipline. Foster writes, "Celebration is central to all the Spiritual Disciplines. Without a joyful spirit of festivity the Disciplines become dull, death-breathing tools in the hands of modern Pharisees. Every Discipline should be characterized by carefree gaiety and a sense of thanksgiving."[52] Celebration is a kind of capstone for all the disciplines we've explored. It can be woven into the other eleven spiritual habits we've already covered.

In another sense, though, celebration stands on its own. We may choose to focus on celebration in its own right as a way of growing in our experience of and expression of joy. Celebration consists of intentional habits and practices designed to heighten our happiness and deepen our delight in Christ. The wonderful thing about this discipline is that almost anything is fair game—even rocks. Best-selling author and speaker Michael Hyatt writes of a friend of his who encouraged him to start carrying around a "gratitude rock."[53] Each time Hyatt felt the rock in his pocket, he was to give thanks to God for whatever was happening at that moment—good or bad. The practice transformed his attitude. Instead of being a glass-is-half-empty person, he became a glass-is-half-full person. He began to experience joy for the good he already had in the present rather than despair for the good he lacked. It was a simple way of learning to celebrate.

TAKE ⑩

Take ten minutes today and do something you really enjoy doing. Give yourself permission to indulge in the satisfaction that choice brings. Give praise to God and express your gratitude to him.

40

Praising in Phases

The Most Overlooked Discipline

Researchers have confirmed what most parents suspected—gratitude is a foreign language learned reluctantly by youngsters. In her book The Gift of Thanks, Margaret Visser cites a study that observed children saying things such as "hi," "thanks," and "good-bye."[54] Kids voluntarily said "hi" 27 percent of the time, "good-bye" 25 percent of the time, and "thanks" 7 percent of the time. Parents had to prompt "hi" 28 percent of the time, "good-bye" 33 percent of the time, and "thanks" 51 percent of the time. Based on this research Visser concludes that thankfulness and gratitude are difficult subjects to master: "In our culture thanksgiving is believed to be, for most children, the very last of basic social graces they acquire... Children have to be 'brought up' to say they are grateful."

Acknowledgments of appreciation are too often last on our children's lips, perhaps because gratitude is a habit of the heart—unlike the social niceties of when to say hi and good-bye. Genuine thankfulness requires an outlook on life that goes beyond seeing ourselves as completely self-reliant, in need of no one, yet entitled to all. Heartfelt thankfulness comes from the understanding that we are dependent on others and entitled to nothing. Even life itself is grace. So our very lives, and all the good they contain, should evoke the response of gratitude, especially to the One who is the Source of all that is good (Jam. 1:17). It takes a good deal of time for children to grasp this, assuming they ever do.

This phenomena explains why Dallas Willard states that celebration (the ultimate "thank you" to God) is one of the "most overlooked and misunderstood" disciplines.[55] Because things such as gratitude are learned lastly (if at all), the spiritual significance of celebration is often lost on us. We are tempted to believe that attention should be given to more "serious" habits such as prayer, fasting, and Bible study. Joy and revelry are too often not thought to be significant signposts on the road of spiritual growth. The result is that not only do youngsters develop gaiety sluggishly but grownups downplay its very importance.

Yet joy is essential to the life imagined by Jesus in his Sermon on the Mount–especially regarding possessions. Jesus encourages us to seek a life ruled by God and not by goods. He pleads with us to invest in things that will outlast our lives. He tells us straight out that it's infinitely better to serve the Father than to serve finances. And joy is one of the ways in which we step in that direction. Joy is the ultimate antidote to avarice, and the greatest catalyst for compassion. As Dallas Willard says, "Celebration heartily done makes our deprivations and sorrows seem small, and we find in it great strength to do the will of our God because his goodness becomes so real to us."[56] We no longer pine for what we do not have, but instead passionately use what we do have for the will of God. Celebration releases us from craving more and makes sharing more possible.

Stage One Gratitude

Author Chuck Colson calls the first step toward joy "natural gratitude." Natural gratitude is the thankfulness that stems from easily recognizable gifts: "Life, health, home, family, freedom, a tall, cold lemonade on a summer day–it's a mindset of active appreciation for all good gifts." These are the gifts that come quickly to mind when we are dwelling "in a world full of…blessings."[57] We might call this stage one gratitude. It is the gratitude that comes instinctively. This praise is prompted by what's obvious: a steady job, good health, a best friend, a great meal, a kind note of appreciation, or a recent prayer answered positively. This is joy generated by what God has done–those things that are clear and obvious to us.

Though this gratitude ought to come naturally, sometimes it doesn't. Richard Foster writes about four obstacles that keep us from stage one joy.[58] The first obstacle is inattention. We simply do not pay attention to good things God has given us. We miss them though they are right in front of our eyes. A second obstacle is the wrong kind of attention. For example, we might pay attention to a sunset. But rather than allowing the sunset to stir us to applause, we allow it to stir us to analysis–why does the sun turn that color, etc.? A third obstacle is greed. Foster writes, "Instead of simply enjoying pleasures, we demand more pleasures–whether we enjoy them or not." The final hindrance is conceit. Conceit leads us to focus on and admire what we have done rather than attend to and appreciate what God has done.

Thus, even when the sun is shining and all seems right in the world, experiencing genuine joy requires the following: (1) opening our eyes and paying attention to the plentiful presents God has placed in front of our noses, (2) adoring the Giver rather than analyzing the gift, (3) choosing satisfaction with what God's already done rather than dissatisfaction for what he has not yet done, and (4) embracing the conviction that it's not our hard work that has filled our hands–it's God's great grace.

Stage Two Gratitude

But joy and praise are even more difficult to acquire when the day seems dark and blessings seem hidden. What happens when we suddenly find ourselves in what Colson calls "the world of brokenness?" Colson writes of another form of joy that becomes necessary:

> [Natural] gratitude doesn't come naturally–if at all–when things go badly. It can't buoy us in difficult times... And, to paraphrase Jesus, even pagans can give thanks when things are going well. [Jonathan] Edwards calls the deeper, primary form of thankfulness "gracious gratitude." It gives thanks not for goods received, but for who God is: for His character–His goodness, love, power, excellencies–regardless of favors received... It is relational, rather than conditional. Though our world may shatter, we are secure in Him... And that, more than any words we might utter, is a powerful witness to our neighbors that God's power is real, and His presence very relevant, even in a world full of brokenness as well as blessings.[59]

Stage one gratitude is centered on "goods received"–what God has done. But when there are no goods to receive, stage two gratitude needs to kick in. This is joy that stems solely from who God is.

We get a glimpse of this second kind of gratitude in Psalm 13. David is caught in a trying time. God doesn't seem to be doing anything. Yet David states, "But I have trusted in your steadfast love" (v. 5a). Though David's world is shattering, he finds security in God. The broad scope of his life with God prompts him to believe that God is filled with steadfast love, even though the narrow picture of the present raises questions about that love. In other words, David focuses more on who God is in the midst of the trial rather than on what God has or hasn't done during the trial. Praise whispers from his lips because he is convinced about the unchanging nature of God. Though the present situation may lead some to conclude otherwise, David still trusts that God is a God of steadfast love. This is stage two gratitude–joy rooted in the identity of God rather than solely in the activity of God.

Stage Three Gratitude

There is, however, one more step we might take in discovering joy in a world of brokenness. Jesus models this step. In Matthew 11, Jesus experiences a series of disappointments. Yet at the end of this disappointing day, he expresses gratitude: "I thank you, Father, Lord of heaven and earth, that you have hidden these things from the wise and understanding and revealed them to little children" (Mt. 11:25). Notice what prompts the "I thank you." First, it flows from who God is (stage two gratitude). Rather than focus on his woeful circumstance, Jesus focuses on his wonderful God. He reminds himself that God is "Father" and "Lord of heaven and earth." These divine characteristics have not changed in spite of the day's circumstance.

But Jesus goes beyond this. He also focuses on what God is doing–in the dark. Even though Jesus finds himself amid circumstances in which God does not appear to be working, he recognizes that God is indeed working. Even in this deep pit, God is "hiding" and "revealing"–"you have hidden these things from the wise and understanding and revealed them to little children." Jesus trusts not just in the nature of God but in the mysterious work of God. He believes God is still present and active in spite of the brokenness around him.

Stage three joy stems from the belief that though God's work is covert, God's work is still in play. Just because we can't see it doesn't mean God isn't doing it. God is active behind the scenes and beneath the surface. And though this activity is concealed, it is still cause for celebration. This is the highest form of celebration.

TAKE ⑩

Take ten minutes today to celebrate one of three things: (1) something obvious that God has recently done that prompts praise (stage one), (2) an aspect of God's character that remains fixed even when all else seems to be fluctuating (stage two), or (3) God's hidden work, which is clouded to your eyes but clear to your mind (stage three).

41

Living Large

We've traveled over a lot of territory during these forty days. So much territory that it may be difficult to recall where we started. Let's review. Do you remember the opening story about Kyle MacDonald?[60] Kyle traded a red paper clip for a house. It took many months and many trades. The paper clip for a pen. The pen for a doorknob. The doorknob for a camping stove. Over time the trades grew. And one day Kyle's red paper clip turned into a home in Kipling, Saskatchewan.

Kyle received something large. He offered something little.

This true story is a parable for spiritual formation.

Jesus taught that the kingdom of heaven might start tiny–like a mustard seed. It would grow, however, into something tremendous–a tree in which birds nest (Mt. 13:31–32). Jesus said people could obtain something massive–like the removal of a mountain–if they gave something minuscule–like faith as small as a mustard seed (Mt. 17:20). Large gift. Little offering.

More than Heaven

But what is this large gift Jesus offers? Christians have often answered that question with one word: heaven. Jesus came to give the huge gift of heaven. But is that all? In his book After You Believe, N. T. Wright tells of James. James was asking this very question:

> James…had been attending the church where he'd had that wonderful, life-changing experience. He had learned a lot about God and Jesus. He'd learned a lot, too, about himself. He had been taught, quite correctly, that God loved him more than he could ever imagine–indeed, so much that God sent

Jesus to die for him. The preachers he had listened to had insisted that nothing we humans do can make us acceptable to God, now or in the ultimate future. Everything is a gift of God's sheer grace and generosity. James had drunk all this in like someone who's walked ten miles on a hot day and is suddenly given a large glass of cold water. It was wonderful news. He was living by it. But he found himself now staring at a big question mark. What am I here for?

He put it like this, as we talked. This is how it stacked up: God loves me; yes. He's transformed my life so that I find I want to pray, to worship, to read the Bible, to abandon the old self-destructive ways I used to behave. That's great. ...And obviously all this comes with the great promise that one day I'll be with God forever. I know I'll die one day, but Jesus has guaranteed that everybody who trusts him will live with him in heaven. That's great too. But what am I here for now? What happens after you believe?

The reason James knocked on my door was that he wasn't satisfied with the answers he'd been getting from his friends and from people in the church he was attending. All they could say was that God called some people to particular spheres of Christian service—into full-time pastoral ministry, for instance, or to be teachers or doctors or missionaries or some combination of these and other similar tasks. But James had no sense that any of that was for him. He was finishing his doctorate in computer science and had all sorts of career options opening up before him. Was all that knowledge and opportunity simply irrelevant to the "spiritual" issues? Was he basically going to be hanging around for a few decades, waiting to die and go to heaven, and in the meantime using some of his spare time to persuade other people to do the same? Was that really it? Isn't there anything else that happens after you believe and before you finally die and go to heaven?[61]

James wasn't trying to belittle the gift of heaven. He was simply wondering if heaven was enough. Was that all Jesus came to give? If so, why are we still here? Why didn't we beam directly to heaven after our baptism?

I think James is right. Jesus offers us a gift larger than just being loved (although it's wonderful to be loved by God!), just practicing religion, just going to heaven, or just becoming ministers or missionaries. Jesus offers more than life after death. He also offers life before death.

Jesus reveals this gift in his Sermon on the Mount. Here Jesus envisions this massive life as a house (Mt. 7:24), and then he describes it. It's a house—that is, a life—larger than we could possibly imagine. The house contains three components.

First, Jesus offers the giant gift of a piety that is genuine. Genuineness is what contemporary critics often find so lacking in faith. For example, David Kinnaman and Gabe Lyons interviewed people ages sixteen to twenty-nine who wanted nothing to do with the Christian faith. They asked these young adults what they thought about Christianity. Again and again they said, "Christians are hypocritical."[62] Hypocrisy is the extreme opposite of genuineness and authenticity. And people today are longing for something larger than hypocrisy.

Jesus offers this gift. He offers a piety, a walk with God that is authentic. In fact, as John Ortberg writes, what set Jesus apart from the religious leaders of his day was his focus on the heart.[63] Jesus emphasized a spirituality of sincerity, one that flowed from the inside-out, one that was not just skin-deep. He waged war against religious ideologies that were satisfied with merely the superficial (see Mt. 23:13, 15, 16, 23, 27, 29). And in his Sermon on the Mount, he provides a path away from hypocrisy and toward authenticity (e.g., Mt. 6:1–6, 16–18).

Second, Jesus offers the giant gift of relationships with people who are gracious. Graciousness is often absent in the relationships formed by religious people today. David Kinnaman's research on those who are leaving churches finds that one of the primary reasons for the exodus is that too many churches are more known for whom they exclude than whom they embrace.[64] They are more likely to ward off people than welcome them. Robin Meyers writes similarly about the irony of those who seem to believe in Christ but refuse to treat people like Jesus.[65] They are filled with Christ-like conviction for the doctrines in the Bible but are not filled with Jesus-like compassion for the people around them. People are longing for something larger than intolerance, hatred, and judgment when it comes to religion.

Jesus offers this gift. He offers a spirituality in which relationships are characterized by graciousness. He teaches kindness, compassion, and love—even for our enemies (e.g., Mt. 5:21–48).

Third, Jesus offers the giant gift of using possessions in ways that are generous. Generosity is often a missing element today, even among the spiritual. Richard Foster writes that "The crying need today is for people of faith to live faithfully. This is true in all spheres of human existence, but it is particularly true with reference to money, sex, and power."[66] He reminds us that "Martin Luther astutely observed, 'There are three conversions necessary: the conversion of the heart, mind, and the purse.'"[67] This final conversion is one that many spiritual people have not undergone.

Jesus makes this conversion central to his faith. In his Sermon, he shows how to live in a right way with resources so that they bless others and honor God. Jesus offers the giant gift of using possessions in ways that are generous (e.g., Mt. 6:22–33).

The life Jesus brings is larger than we can imagine. It's not just pie-in-the-sky-by-and-by. It's about experiencing a heart-to-heart relationship with God, building relationships that make a difference, and using resources to bring joy to others. All right here and right now.

Paper Clips

And the steps into that life may be smaller than we've dreamed. Like the paper clip turned into a home, our tiny offerings of ten-minute disciplines can be used by God to lead us to this tremendous life.

For forty days you've experienced twelve of these ten-minute disciplines. But the journey's just begun. As you close this book, my hope is that you're opening the door to a whole new relationship with God. My wish is that you not only continue in your ten-minute disciplines but that you expand them until each minute of every day is devoted to the Sermon-on-the-Mount-life. The more this life becomes your life, the more—Jesus promises—you'll become the salt of the earth and light of the world (Mt. 5:13–15). God will use you to drive out darkness and decay. And the result will be that more and more people will shout "Glory to God!" (Mt. 5:16). Your life will inspire others to experience a similar life.

TAKE ⑩

So take just one more ten-minute time block and consider your answer to two questions. First, which of the twelve spiritual disciplines in this book are you most passionate about? Which one truly engages your heart? Which one makes you excited when you remember practicing it in the preceding weeks?

Second, what could you do to expand your experience of this discipline? What steps could you take to spend twenty minutes, an hour, or entire days in this habit? It's time to trade-up. It's time to turn in that paper clip for a doorknob, and the doorknob for a generator, and the generator for a snowmobile. Turn this final page with a plan for making that one spiritual habit a greater part of your life.

Appendix

In chapter 8 I described three types of Psalms: Psalms from the Plain, Psalms from the Pit, and Psalms from the Peak. In the chart below you will find all 150 Psalms placed into one of these categories. When you read or pray through the Psalms, you might want to keep this chart close by. It will help you identify the type of psalm and know better how to use it in your prayer life.

Prayers from the Plain	Prayers from the Pit	Prayers from the Peak
Ps. 1	Ps. 2	Ps. 11
8	3	16
14	4	18
15	5	20
19	6	21
24	7	23
33	9	27
37	10	29
49	12	30
78	13	34
104	17	45
105	22	46
106	25	47
112	26	48
119:1–16	28	62
119:17–24	31	63

Prayers from the Plain	Prayers from the Pit	Prayers from the Peak
119:25–32	32	65
119:33–40	35	66
119:41–48	36	67
119:49–56	38	68
119:57–64	39	72
119:65–72	40	75
119:73–80	41	76
119:81–88	42	84
119:89–96	43	87
119:97–104	44	91
119:105–112	50	92
119:113–120	51	93
119:121-128	52	95
119:129–136	53	96
119:137–144	54	97
119:145–152	55	98
119:153–160	56	99
119:161–168	57	100
119:169–176	58	101
127	59	103
128	60	107
133	61	110
135	64	111
136	69	113
145	70	114
	71	115

Prayers from the Plain	Prayers from the Pit	Prayers from the Peak
	73	116
	74	117
	77	118
	79	121
	80	122
	81	124
	82	125
	83	131
	85	132
	86	134
	88	138
	89	144
	90	146
	94	147
	102	148
	108	149
	109	150
	120	
	123	
	126	
	129	
	130	
	137	
	139	
	140	
	141	

184 Ten-Minute Transformation

Prayers from the Plain	Prayers from the Pit	Prayers from the Peak
	142	
	143	

Notes

Section One: Living on Purpose

1 Joseph L. Cannon, "For Missionaries Only" (New Zealand: The Last Stop Printing Service, 1994); online PDF http://www.harding.edu/cwm/archives/resources/books/FOR_MISSIONARIES_ONLY.PDF

2 Mother Teresa, as quoted in Alan Hirsch and Lance Ford, *Right Here, Right Now* (Grand Rapids, Mich.: Baker Books, 2011), Kindle edition location 478.

3 Kyle MacDonald, *One Red Paperclip* (New York: Three Rivers Press, 2007).

4 Alicia Chang, Associated Press, "Daily exercise of 15 minutes helps," Memphis, *The Commercial Appeal,* 21 August 2001, A10.

5 From http://www.gladwell.com/1996/1996_06_03_a_tipping.htm.

6 Ibid.

7 Average includes those who spend no time at all; Ted Olsen, "Go Figure," *Christianity Today* (August 2010): 13; based on a report from Bureau of Labor Statistics (http://www.bls.gov/news.release/atus.t01.htm).

8 See Chris Altrock, *Rebuilding Relationships* (St. Louis, Mo.: Chalice Press, 2008) for an in-depth look at how the Sermon on the Mount covers these three areas.

9 Dallas Willard, *Renovation of the Heart* (Colorado Springs: NavPress, 2002); id., "Living a Transformed Life Adequate to Our Calling," http://www.dwillard.org/articles/printable.asp?artid+119.

10 Daniel Pink, *Drive: The Surprising Truth about What Motives Us* (New York: Riverhead Press, 2011).

11 From http://ww.danpink.com/archives/2011/01/whats-your-sentence-the-video.

12 "The Pastors' Connection" (Open Doors USA e-mail, August 2002); corroborated by Kelly Callaghan, prayer and courier coordinator for Open Doors USA.

13 Karl Rahner, quoted in Don Posteroski and Gary Nelson, *Future Faith Churches: Reconnecting with the Power of the Gospel for the 21st Century* (Ketowna, British Columbia: Wood Lake, 1997), 10.

14 http://www.washingtontimes.com/news/2011/feb/9/crucifying-chinas-christians/.

15 Warren Bennis and Burt Nanus, *Leaders,* 2d ed. (New York: HarperBusiness, 2007), 66–72.

16 Dallas Willard, Jan Johnson, and Keith Matthews, *Dallas Willard's Guide to The Divine Conspiracy* (San Francisco: HarperSanFrancisco, 2001), 107.

17 John Ortberg, "True (and False) Transformation," *Leadership* (Summer 2002): 104.

18 Inspired by Stephen R. Covey, A. Roger Merrill, and Rebecca R. Merrill, *First Things First* (New York: Free Press, 1996), 15ff.

19 Daniel Levitin, as quoted in Malcolm Gladwell, *Outliers: The Story of Success* (New York: Little, Brown and Company, 2008), 40.

20 Willard, et al., *Guide to The Divine Conspiracy,* 107.

21 John Ortberg, *The Life You've Always Wanted* (Grand Rapids, Mich.: Zondervan, 1997), 48.

Section Two: Genuine in Piety

1 Richard Foster, *Celebration of Discipline,* rev. ed. (New York: Harper & Row, 1978), 1.

2 Adele Calhoun, *Spiritual Disciplines Handbook* (Downers Grove, Ill.: InterVarsity Press, 2005), 52.

3 From http://religion.blogs.cnn.com/2011/03/21/why-do-muslims-pray-five-times-daily/ .

4 Brother Lawrence and Frank Laubach, *Practicing His Presence,* The Library of Spiritual Classics, vol. 1 (Jacksonville, Fla.: SeedSowers Christian Publishing, 1988), 91.

5 David L. Fleming, *What Is Ignatian Spirituality?* (Chicago: Loyola Press, 2008), 21–22.

6 Dominic Gates, "Boeing Field beads damage new jet engines," *Seattle Times,* 18 December 2004, http://seattletimes.com/html/businesstechnology/2002123625_boeingfield18.html.

7 Richard Foster, *Prayer: Finding the Heart's True Home* (San Francisco: HarperSanFrancisco, 1992), 27.

8 Ibid., 27–28.

9 St. Ignatius Loyola and Father Elder Mullan, *The Spiritual Exercises of St. Ignatius of Loyola* (Charlotte, N.C.: Saint Benedict Press, 2010), 21–22.

10 John Ortberg, *The Life You've Always Wanted* (Grand Rapids, Mich.: Zondervan, 1997), 123–24.

11 Ibid., 126.

12 Marjorie Thompson, *Soul Feast: An Invitation to the Christian Spiritual Life* (Louisville: Westminster John Knox, 1995), 86.

13 Ibid., 98–99.

14 Ruth Haley Barton, *Sacred Rhythms Participant's Guide* (Grand Rapids, Mich.: Zondervan, 2011), 62.

15 Mark Thibodeaux, *Armchair Mystic* (Cincinnati: Saint Anthony Messenger Press, 2001), 53.

16 Calhoun, *Spiritual Disciplines Handbook,* 246.

17 See Walter Brueggemann, *The Message of the Psalms* (Minneapolis: Augsburg, 1984) and *Spirituality of the Psalms* (Minneapolis: Fortress, 2002).

18 Peter Kreeft, *Prayer for Beginners* (San Francisco: Ignatius, 2000), 25–26.

19 Kevin Sullivan and Joe Wiesenfeld (screen adaptation), *Anne of Green Gables,* directed by Kevin Sullivan (1985, Canadian Broadcasting Company; Walt Disney Home Video, 1986), based on a novel by Lucy Maud Montgomery

20 See Chris Altrock, *Prayers from the Pit* (Nashville: 21st Century Christian, 2011).

21 For an explanation of why this line from Jesus should be considered a prayer, see ibid., chapter 10.

22 Foster, *Prayer,* 107–108.

23 Eva Hermann, as quoted in John Ortberg, *The Me I Want to Be* (Grand Rapids, Mich.: Zondervan, 2010), 111.

24 Calhoun, *Spiritual Disciplines Handbook,* 240.

25 Jan Johnson, *When the Soul Listens* (Colorado Springs: NavPress, 1999), 52. (Deut. 29:4; Ps. 115:6; 135:17; Prov. 20:12; Isa. 6:10; 30:21; 32:3; 42:20; Jer. 5:21; 6:10; 9:20; Ezek. 12:2; 40:4; Mt. 11:15; 13:9, 15–16, 43; Mk. 4:9, 23; 8:18; Lk. 8:8; 14:35; Acts 28:27; Rom. 11:8)

26 See Richard Foster, *Celebration of Discipline,* 20th Anniversary Edition (San Francisco: HarperSanFrancisco, 1998), 15–17.

27 Tony Jones, *The Sacred Way* (Grand Rapids, Mich.: Zondervan, 2005), 48.

28 Ibid., 49–50.

29 Bill Hybels, *The Power of a Whisper* (Grand Rapids, Mich.: Zondervan, 2010), Kindle edition.

30 Marjorie Thompson, *Soul Feast* (Louisville: Westminster John Knox, 1985), 18 (*emphasis added*).

32 Mark Buchanan, *Your God Is Too Safe* (Sisters, Oreg.: Multnomah, 2001), 204.

32 Priscilla Shirer, *Discerning the Voice of God* (Chicago: Moody, 2007), 19–20.

33 Richard Foster, *Celebration of Discipline,* rev. ed. (New York: Harper & Row, 1978), 29 (*emphasis mine.*

34 Holly Pevzner, "Silence," *Real Simple* (July 2011).

35 Gordon Hempton and John Grossmann, *One Square Inch of Silence* (New York: Free Press, 2009), 1.

36 Richard J. Foster, *Sanctuary of the Soul: Journey into Meditative Prayer* (Downers Grove, Ill.: InterVarsity Press, 2011), 104.

37 George Prochnik, "Now don't hear this," Opinion, *The New York Times,* 2 May 2010, WK11. http://www.nytimes.com/2010/05/02/opinion/02prochnik.html.

38 See Thomas Keating, *Open Mind, Open Heart,* 20th Anniversary Deluxe Edition (New York: Continuum, 2006).

39 Ibid.

40 Carl McColman, *The Big Book of Christian Mysticism* (Charlottesville, Va.: Hampton Roads, 2010), 236.

41 Foster, *Celebration of Discipline,* 20.

42 Ruth Haley Barton and Dallas Willard, *Invitation to Solitude and Silence* (Downers Grove, Ill.: InterVarsity Press, 2010), 29–30.

43 Keating, *Open Mind, Open Heart,* 141.

44 Thibodeaux, *Armchair Mystic,* 153.

45 Keating, *Open Mind, Open Heart,* 47.

46 Quoted in Thomas Merton, *Contemplative Prayer* (Colorado Springs: Image Books, 1996), 59.

47 Ibid., 42.

48 Keating, *Open Mind, Open Heart,* 47.

49 Jones, *The Sacred Way,* 39–40.

50 Gary Holloway, *You Might Be Too Busy If…Spiritual Practices for People in a Hurry* (Abilene, Tex.: Leafwood Publishers, 2009), 41.

51 Calhoun, *Spiritual Disciplines Handbook,* 108.

52 Foster, *Prayer,* 158.

53 Calhoun, *Spiritual Disciplines Handbook,* 107.

54 Keating, *Open Mind, Open Heart,* 37.

55 Holloway, *You Might Be Too Busy If...,* 46–47.

56 Calhoun, *Spiritual Disciplines Handbook,* 109.

57 Holloway, *You Might Be Too Busy If...,* 46–47.

58 Merton, *Contemplative Prayer,* 34.

Section Three: Gracious toward People

1 Tony Jones, *The Sacred Way* (Grand Rapids, Mich.: Zondervan, 2005), 193.

2 Dallas Willard, *The Spirit of the Disciplines* (San Francisco: HarperSanFrancisco, 1988), 182.

3 Mark Buchanan, *Your God Is Too Safe* (Sisters:Oreg.: Multnomah, 2001), 211–12.

4 Richard Foster, *Celebration of Discipline,* rev. ed. (New York: Harper & Row, 1978), 130.

5 Willard, *The Spirit of the Disciplines,* 172–73.

6 James Bryan Smith, *The Good and Beautiful Life* (Downers Grove, Ill.: InterVarsity Press, 2009), 139.

7 John Ortberg, *The Life You've Always Wanted* (Grand Rapids, Mich.: Zondervan, 1997), 109–18.

8 Adele Calhoun, *Spiritual Disciplines Handbook* (Downers Grove, Ill.: InterVarsity Press, 2005), 146, 185.

9 Foster, *Celebration of Discipline,* 128–29.

10 Rebecca Pippert, *Hope Has Its Reasons* (Downers Grove, Ill.: InterVarsity Press, 2001), 31–32.

11 Ibid.

12 Smith, *The Good and Beautiful Life,* 188.

13 Ibid., 185–201.

14 Marjorie Thompson, *Soul Feast* (Louisville: Westminster John Knox, 1995), 98.

15 Adi Ignatius, "We Had to Own the Mistakes," *Harvard Business Review* (July-August 2010): 109.

16 John Ortberg, *The Me I Want to Be* (Grand Rapids, Mich.: Zondervan, 2010), 146.

17 Foster, *Celebration of Discipline,* 153.

18 Buchanan, *Your God Is Too Safe,* 166–67.

19 Mark R. McMinn, *Why Sin Matters* (Wheaton, Ill.: Tyndale, 2004), 14.

20 Adapted from Thompson, *Soul Feast,* 96–97.

21 Smith, *The Good and Beautiful Community,* 19.

22 Ortberg, *The Life You've Always Wanted,* 82.

23 "Survey: Christians Worldwide Too Busy for God," www.christianpost.com

24 Based on Ortberg, *The Life You've Always Wanted,* 84–88.

25 Ibid., 87.

26 Buchanan, *Your God Is Too Safe,* 187.

27 Mike Yaconelli, *Messy Spirituality* (Grand Rapids, Mich.: Zondervan, 2007), 95.

28 Joseph Bailey, *Slowing Down to the Speed of Love* (New York: McGraw Hill, 2004).

29 Ortberg, *The Life You've Always Wanted,* 89; Calhoun, *Spiritual Disciplines Handbook,* 81.

30 Gary Holloway, *You Might Be Too Busy If...Spiritual Practices for People in a Hurry* (Abilene, Tex.: Leafwood, 2009), 65–66.

31 Ibid.

32 Richard Foster, *Prayer: Finding the Heart's True Home* (San Francisco: HarperSanFrancisco, 1992), 191.

33 Thompson, *Soul Feast,* 37.

34 Douglas Steere, as quoted in ibid., 37.

35 Foster, *Prayer,* 191.

36 George A. Buttrick, *So We Believe, So We Pray* (Nashville: Abingdon, 1951), 121.

37 William Willimon and Stanley Hauerwas, *Lord, Teach Us* (Nashville: Abingdon, 1996), 18.

38 From Frederick Buechner, *Listening to Your Life* (San Francisco: HarperSanFrancisco, 1992), quoted in ibid., 9.

39 Mike Breem and Steve Cockram, *Building a Discipling Culture* (Pawleys, S.C.: 3DM, 2011), Kindle location 2051.

40 David Buttrick, *Speaking Jesus* (Louisville: Westminster John Knox, 2002), 143.

41 Gordon MacDonald, "Praying That Makes a Difference," *Leadership Journal* (Spring 2012): 91–94.

42 Foster, *Celebration of Discipline,* 39.

43 Ibid., 44.

44 Willard, *The Spirit of the Disciplines,* 185–86.

45 Smith, *The Good and Beautiful Life,* 119–36.

Section Four: Generous with Possessions

1 Richard Foster, *Money, Sex, and Power* (New York: Harper & Row, 1985), 20–23.

2 Adele Calhoun, *Spiritual Disciplines Handbook* (Downers Grove, Ill.: InterVarsity Press, 2005), 138.

3 Dallas Willard, *The Spirit of the Disciplines,* (New York: Harper Collins, 1988), 194–96.

4 Henri Nouwen, *Reaching Out: The Three Movements of the Spiritual Life* (Colorado Springs: Image, 1975), 66.

5 Christine D. Pohl, *Making Room: Recovering Hospitality as a Christian Tradition* (Grand Rapids, Mich.: Eerdmans, 1999), 6–7.

6 Marjorie Thompson, *Soul Feast* (Louisville: Westminster John Knox, 1995), 122.

7 Ibid., 129–35.

8 Nouwen, *Reaching Out.*

9 Rodney K. Duke, "Hospitality," *Baker's Evangelical Dictionary of Biblical Theology,* ed. Walter A. Elwell (Grand Rapids, Mich.: Baker Books, 1996).

10 Christine D. Pohl, *Making Room,* 20–31.

11 Ibid., 30.

12 James Bryan Smith, *The Good and Beautiful Community* (Downers Grove, Ill.: InterVarsity Press, 2010), 149–53.

13 Brother Lawrence and Frank Laubach, *Practicing His Presence,* The Library of Spiritual Classics, vol. 1 (Jacksonville, Fla.: SeedSowers Christian Publishing, 1988).

14 Ibid., 60.

15 Ibid., 55.

16 Ibid., 76, 78.

17 Ibid., 76.

18 Ibid., 91.

19 Derek Thompson, "The 100-Year March of Technology in 1 Graph," *The Atlantic,* 7 April 2012, www.theatlantic.com.

20 Brother Lawrence and Laubach, *Practicing His Presence,* 10.

21 Ibid., 2.

22 Ibid.

23 Ibid., 14.

24 Ibid., 31–35; Calhoun, *Spiritual Disciplines Handbook,* 61.

25 D. A. Carson, "Athens Revisited," in *Telling the Truth,* ed. D. A. Carson (Grand Rapids, Mich.: Zondervan, 2000), 386–89.

26 Richard Foster, *Prayer: Finding the Heart's True Home* (San Francisco: HarperSanFrancisco, 1992), 119.

27 Mark Buchanan, *Your God Is Too Safe* (Sisters, Oreg.: Multnomah, 2001), 141.

28 Mark Buchanan, *Things Unseen: Living with Eternity in Your Heart* (Sisters, Oreg.: Multnomah, 2006), 50–51.

29 This is why the letters are known as "pastorals." See Walter L. Liefeld, *1 and 2 Timothy, Titus,* The NIV Application Commentary (Grand Rapids, Mich.: Zondervan, 2011), Kindle location 274.

30 Foster, *Money, Sex, and Power,* 5–7, 71–87.

31 Thom S. Rainer and Art Rainer, *Simple Life* (Nashville: B & H Publishing, 2009), 24.

32 Ibid., 24–25.

33 Simple suggestions are compiled from the following sources: Richard Foster, *Freedom of Simplicity* (San Francisco: HarperOne, 2005); Elaine St. James, *Simplify Your Life* (New York: Hyperion, 1994); H. Norman Wright, *Simplify Your Life And Get More Out of It!* (Wheaton, Ill.: Tyndale, 1998); Richard Foster, "The Discipline of Simplicity," in *Simpler Living, Compassionate Life,* ed. Michael Schut (Denver: Living the Good News, 1999), 180–89; John Ortberg, *The Life You've Always Wanted* (Grand Rapids, Mich.: Zondervan, 1997); Kim Thomas, *Simplicity* (Nashville: Broadman & Holman, 1999).

34 Michael Schut, "The Good Life and the Abundant Life," in *Simpler Living, Compassionate Life,* 24–26.

35 James Dobson, *Dr. Dobson's Handbook of Family Advice* (Eugene, Oreg.: Harvest House, 1996), 213.

36 C. S. Lewis, *Mere Christianity* (New York: Touchstone, 1980), 139–40.

37 Donald S. Whitney, *Simplify Your Spiritual Life: Spiritual Disciplines for the Overwhelmed* (Colorado Springs: NavPress, 2003), 140.

38 Richard Foster, *Celebration of Discipline,* rev. ed. (New York: Harper & Row, 1978), 88–89.

39 Simple suggestions are compiled from the sources listed in note 33.?]

40 Donna Schaper, "Traveling Light on New Year's Eve," *Christian Science Monitor* (12-31-97), http://www.csmonitor.com/1997/1231/123197.home.home.1.html.

41 Gary Holloway, *You Might Be Too Busy If…Spiritual Practices for People in a Hurry* (Abilene, Tex.: Leafwood, 2009), 63–72.

42 Richard Foster, *Freedom of Simplicity,* 108–109.

43 Simple suggestions are compiled from the sources listed in note 33..

44 "The Dick Staub Interview: Brennan Manning on Ruthless Trust," ChristianityToday.com (12-10-02).

45 Elesha Coffman, quoting John McRay, "Stench, Pain, and Misery," *Christian History* (Issue 47). Available through christianhistoryinstitute.org.

46 Gerald F. Hawthorne, *Philippians,* Word Biblical Commentary (Nashville: Thomas Nelson, 1983), 200.

47 James Strong, *The Exhaustive Concordance of the Bible: Showing Every Word of the Text of the Common English Version of the Canonical Books, and Every Occurrence of Each Word in Regular Order,* electronic ed. (Ontario: Woodside Bible Fellowship, 1996), G842.

48 Foster, *Celebration of Discipline,* 197–200.

49 Ibid., 196.

50 From http://www.jonascuff.com/stuffchristianslike/2011/05/the-miserable-god/?utm_source=feedburner&utm_medium=feed&utm_campaign=Feed%3A+s tuffchristianslikeblog+%28Stuff+Christians+Like+-+Jon+Acuff%29.

51 Dennis Prager, *Happiness Is a Serious Problem* (New York: Regan Books, 1998), 4.

52 Foster, *Celebration of Discipline,* 191.

53 From http://michaelhyatt.com/practicing-the-attitude-of-gratitude.html?utm_ source=feedburner&utm_medium=feed&utm_campaign+Feed%3Amichaelhyatt +%28Michael+Hyatt%29&utm_content=Google+Feedfetcher.

54 Margaret Visser, *The Gift of Thanks* (Boston: Houghton Mifflin Harcourt, 2009), 8–15.

55 Willard, *The Spirit of the Disciplines,* 179.

56 Ibid., 181.

57 Chuck Colson, "Grateful for God in Tough Times," *Christian Post* (July 5, 2011), www.christianpost.com; _ Colson is using categories from preacher/theologian Jonathan Edwards.

58 Foster, *Prayer,* 85–87.

59 Colson, "Grateful for God in Tough Times."

60 Kyle MacDonald, *One Red Paperclip* (Three Rivers Press, 2007).

61 N. T. Wright, *After You Believe* (HarperOne, 2012), 1–3.

62 David Kinnaman and Gabe Lyons, *UnChristian: What a New Generation Really Thinks about Christianity… and Why It Matters* (Baker, 2007), 41.

63 John Ortberg *Who is This Man?* (Zondervan, 2012), 119.

64 David Kinnaman, *You Lost Me* (Baker Books, 2011), 179.

65 Robin Meyers, *Saving Jesus from the Church* (HarperOne, 2010), 6, 14.

66 Richard Foster, *Money, Sex & Power* (Harper & Row, 1985), 1.

67 Ibid., 19.